A PLUME BOOK

FIERCE FOOD

CHRISTA WEIL is the author of *Secondhand Chic*. Before publishing her first book, she lived in Paris, where she was a restaurant reviewer for the *Paris Free Voice*, the city's premier English-language magazine. She has also written articles on food and culture for various publications. She lives in London, England.

THE INTREPID DINER'S GUIDE TO THE UNUSUAL, EXOTIC, AND DOWNRIGHT BIZARRE

FIERCE FOOD

CHRISTA WEIL

A PLUME BOOK

PLUME
Published by Penguin Group
Penguin Group (USA) Inc., 375 Hudson Street, New York, New York 10014,
U.S.A. • Penguin Group (Canada), 90 Eglinton Avenue East, Suite 700,
Toronto, Ontario, Canada M4P 2Y3 (a division of Pearson Penguin Canada Inc.)
• Penguin Books Ltd., 80 Strand, London WC2R 0RL, England • Penguin
Ireland, 25 St. Stephen's Green, Dublin 2, Ireland (a division of Penguin Books
Ltd.) • Penguin Group (Australia), 250 Camberwell Road, Camberwell, Victoria
3124, Australia (a division of Pearson Australia Group Pty. Ltd.) • Penguin
Books India Pvt. Ltd., 11 Community Centre, Panchsheel Park, New Delhi –
110 017, India • Penguin Books (NZ), cnr Airborne and Rosedale Roads,
Albany, Auckland 1310, New Zealand (a division of Pearson New Zealand Ltd.)
• Penguin Books (South Africa) (Pty.) Ltd., 24 Sturdee Avenue, Rosebank,
Johannesburg 2196, South Africa

Penguin Books Ltd., Registered Offices: 80 Strand, London WC2R 0RL, England

First published by Plume, a member of Penguin Group (USA) Inc.

First Printing, October 2006
10   9   8   7   6   5   4   3   2   1

 REGISTERED TRADEMARK—MARCA REGISTRADA

LIBRARY OF CONGRESS CATALOGING-IN-PUBLICATION DATA
Weil, Christa.
   Fierce food : the intrepid diner's guide to the unusual, exotic, and downright
bizarre / By Christa Weil.
      p. cm.
   "A Plume Book."
   ISBN 0-452-28700-6 (trade pbk.)
1. Cookery, International.   2. Food habits.   3. Cookery—Humor.   I. Title.
   TX725.A1W372   2006
   641.59—dc22
                                                                        2006010245

Printed in the United States of America
Set in Cochin

PUBLISHER'S NOTE
Every effort has been made to ensure that the information contained in this book is
complete and accurate. However, neither the publisher nor the author is engaged in
rendering professional advice or services to the individual reader. The ideas, proce-
dures, and suggestions contained in this book are not intended as a substitute for
consulting with your physician. All matters regarding your health require medical
supervision. Neither the author nor the publisher shall be liable or responsible for
any loss or damage allegedly arising from any information or suggestion in this book.

To Dean with love

ACKNOWLEDGMENTS

First and most important, I would like to thank the harvesters, preparers, and cooks who have made these extraordinary eating experiences possible.

So many people have been so generous with their time and thoughts . . . I'd like to send special thanks to William Rubel, Todd Dalton, Richard Weller, Christine Whitacre, the PU alums of Colombia, Andrew Dalby, Fergus Henderson, Debra McCown, Eric Sanford, Susana Trilling, Pablo Raul, Gerald Callahan, Daniel Winkler, Chris R. Calkins, David Mohammed, Nobuyoshi Kuraoka, Randy Morgan, Mark Kristal, Richard Hosking, Nicholas Tyler, Matthew Cobb, Russell Bonduriansky, Eric Franks, Paul Levy, Jill Norman, Jane Levi, Clare Ferguson, Shane Pym, Mike Paterniti, George and Anna Catranis, Zona Spray Starks, Jukka Annala, Sam and Adam Kilgour, Nori Okazaki, Thomas and Natsuno Ogawa, Greg Szulgit, Tom Kearney, Christopher Mellqvist, Rick West, Chris Spina, Ed Burlingame, Mike Maki, and, for their inspiration, the organizers and symposiasts at the Oxford Symposium on Food and Cookery.

To my family, for their support and patience: Alexander and Niko, Mom and Dad, Yiayia and Papou, Uli and Claudia, and Kimon Menegas. Thanks so much as well to Andrea Strbova and Ana Maria Cuevas.

I owe much to my agent, Kathy Green, for her unfailing belief and encouragement, and to Whitney Lee. David Cashion has been a wonderful editor, and I am also grateful for the efforts of the behind-the-scenes team at Plume.

Thanks too to Keith Wynn, Dave Thomasson of Spearo UK Ltd, and Felicia, Tanya, Dana, Ladan, Indrani, Allison, Stephanie, Manal, and Michele, who really didn't want to know, but listened anyway.

CONTENTS

KEY

Symbol	Meaning	Symbol	Meaning
✳	Spiny	📖	Requires special technique
☹	Revolting	໌}	Incredibly smelly
⦂	Messy	⊙	Has eyes
💣	Eating may cause pain/disease/death	↗	Aphrodisiac
✂	Requires special equipment	🐾	Tastes like chicken

INTRODUCTION

Most of the time, what we really want to eat, whether we think about it consciously or not, is comfort food. A meal or a snack that's going to taste nice and fill us up with no special effort on our part. And—this is key—no surprises. At the frazzled end of a long day, or the murky beginnings of a new one, we crave food that soothes: easy to eat, tasty, satisfying. The last thing we want is a meal that's going to give us a hard time.

But every so often, we find ourselves contemplating a dish that isn't same-old same-old. Maybe on vacation, when everything's different. Or after the third night of takeout in a row. Or at the urging of other people around the table. At a fair or festival. At times like these, we remember that food can actually thrill: concentrate the mind, sharpen the senses, and offer a richly nuanced tour of the unknown. All in the space of a tablespoon.

This is what fierce food is all about. It provides an extraordinary eating experience, it is food that commands attention. At its most benign it is delicious but unusual, like honeycomb or green coconut. More exotically, it might present a challenging texture, for example blubber, or an off-putting appearance, like geoduck clam. At the far end of the spectrum, it can be outright terrifying, like tarantula. Fierce food turns eating into a form of extreme sport, in which we face down our misgivings and dare to plunge into the unknown. We may not always like what we taste, but the experience of having tasted—of overcoming apprehension about trying something new—is not only life-enhancing, it, like any other kind of adventure, makes for a great story.

Fierce food has been around since long before the reality shows began serving contestants bugs out of a big glass jar. Insects, bizarre fruit, incredible sea creatures, and still-beating organs are regular menu items in many parts of the world. Some of these foods get attention only through anthropologists' field notes. Others are the well-kept secrets of hard-core foodies, the kind of people who hack through a malarial jungle with a machete in one hand and a fork in the other if there's the promise of an outrageous tidbit at the end of the trail. But now, thanks to a shrinking globe and a growing sense of "been there, done that" with mainstream ethnic cuisine, ordinary people are checking out the wilder side of the world's cafeteria. Whether it's the heart-racing appeal of a sensory challenge, or the desire to go deep into a local culture, or the very basic, very human urge to try something new, more and more people are willing to try deeply weird food.

If your idea of high-risk eating is a Wendy's limited-time-only sandwich, this is probably not a book for you. But if you have an adventurous streak, you will be intrigued by the many survival foods featured in *Fierce Food*, from bark to fresh sheep's blood to grubs. How to find them, how to prepare them, how to eat them, even how to enjoy them while you're marooned on that island, crawling through that desert, hauling your indomitable ass across that frozen tundra.

Or maybe you're working in a job that involves business dinners—business dinners that feature dishes like toxic blowfish, guinea pig, or barbecued sheep's head. Are you going to wuss out, blow a potential deal and your own reputation? A gauntlet has been thrown. Few things give locals more pleasure than watching an outsider struggle with a homegrown dish. So there you are, and it's showtime. Are you cool enough to maneuver the food into your mouth and swallow with a smile, or will you flinch, fumble, and grimace it down? Sometimes you just gotta eat it, and if that's the case, you might as well look good. Dignity counts. With this book under your belt, you will have insider knowledge of what a given local delicacy is and exactly what it tastes like—and you can eat it assured that in 95 percent of the cases, it won't be nearly as bad as it looks.

Some regularly eaten foods only look terrifying. Others go the extra mile with their potential for wreaking havoc on your health. News flash: contrary to the images shown in loving close-up on reality shows, it is usually a terrible idea to eat a raw, squirming bug. *Fierce Food* details why. It also describes how to avoid spines, mandibles, psychoactive elements, and toxins that might lead to dessert off a hospital tray, if you actually make it that far.

It's easy (and fun) to linger on the scarier aspects of fierce food, but many of the seventy-two items described here are deeply alluring, as long as you can relax and give in to their charms. Sea urchin gonads, better known as uni, are an exquisite food. Huitlacoche, a fungus that grows on corn, is a Mexican delicacy that looks like hell but tastes deeply, richly good. A fair number of the foods featured are said to have aphrodisiac qualities. This is hardly surprising, since eating anything new — seeing it, smelling it, opening yourself up to new tastes and textures on the tongue — is one of the most sensual experiences you can have with your clothes on.

And, despite the diverse perils and pleasures posed by certain fierce foods, the category as a whole provides an unusually healthy menu. With very few exceptions, these are all-natural, organic, free-range, healthy-fat, high-protein, high-fiber, minimally processed foods. Their molecules have not been tweaked by food scientists to make them more consistent or more crowd-pleasing, and their packaging does not involve clamshells, unless we're talking about actual clams. Lacking preservatives, they don't travel well, which is why you haven't heard of many of them. They are the items our species grew strong on, back when obesity was an aberration and you didn't need an SUV to run down a deer.

The seventy-two entries that follow provide detailed descriptions of how to eat a given item with appreciation, dignity, relative safety, and comprehension of the tradition that put it on the plate. The list is not comprehensive. One reason: it's impossible to catalog every bug, beast, and slime mold that people will swallow in the name of staying alive. Another: some foods, while certainly out there in terms of unusualness or yuck factor, don't merit long discussion. Tripe, tongue, brains, and kidneys pretty much speak for themselves, and there really is no need to say more.

Each of the foods described here poses its own particular set of problems. To help you pinpoint them at a glance, the entries are accompanied by quick-reference icons. The key is as follows:

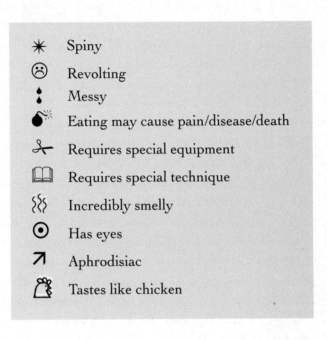

✳	Spiny
☹	Revolting
⁝	Messy
💣	Eating may cause pain/disease/death
✂	Requires special equipment
📖	Requires special technique
∬	Incredibly smelly
⊙	Has eyes
↗	Aphrodisiac
🐔	Tastes like chicken

While every effort has been made to provide accurate information, this food is not called fierce for nothing. What this book can do is provide a good read. What it cannot do is guarantee that:

You'll like it
You won't lose it
Fugu and/or wild mushrooms and/or some other fool
    thing you put in your mouth won't kill you
Foods billed as an aphrodisiac will actually work

Common sense is always important when trying a new food. If you are allergic to shellfish, it is possible you will experience a reaction if you eat an insect. Live insects—particularly those with hard exoskeletons—may contain parasites. Unless it were a matter of survival, I would never eat a raw insect, given the potential aftermath. If you are allergic to eggs, eating balut would not be a wise course of action. If your bowels bloat with gas at the mere sight of cow's milk, you're unlikely to get a free ride with fermented mare's milk, etc., etc.

I have tried two-thirds of the foods listed here and, with a few significant exceptions, plan on working my way through most of the rest of the list. If I had to pin down a single favorite rationale for eating fierce food, it would be the way it takes you back to the raw thrills and chills of childhood—the unfamiliar tastes, the unexpected textures, the uncertain grip on utensils, the question mark of whether you'll like it or not. In the beginning, we all thrive on the ultimate comfort food, mother's milk, or the formula equivalent. The years that follow are one big experiment in oral sensation, but it tends to shut down once we reach adulthood. This book is an argument for opening up once again. Go on. Just a little bite.

FIERCE
FOOD

Armadillo

Back in the 1930s, armadillo was such a frequently eaten fixture of rural southern cuisine that it was called "Hoover hog" in honor of the president who saw America into the Great Depression. Nowadays, it's a lot harder to find eatin' armadillo. Occasionally it turns up as a novelty chili or barbecue meat at fairs in Texas and Arkansas. If you're willing to go farther afield, the Yu Ne Nisa restaurant in Oaxaca, Mexico, cooks it along with other New World specialties like iguana and grasshopper. Armadillo is fun to try and fairly low-risk to taste, as long as it's been thoroughly stewed. All the same, it is just as well that the creature is no longer the everyday fare it once was. The animal is tasty, as fine-grained and flavorsome as pork, but a certain microbe likes it a lot too. Armadillo is the only creature besides man that carries leprosy, a disease that will happily jump species if given the opportunity, for instance when undercooked armadillo flesh meets a small cut in the mouth.

Now known as Hansen's disease, leprosy is a scourge

whose carriers in times past were often stoned out of the village by their friends and neighbors. The lepers banded together in isolated colonies deep in the jungle or on barren islands. Left untreated, the disease ravages fingers, noses, and ears, which eventually rot and drop off altogether. These parts are the first to go because the bacteria thrives in the cooler body temperature of the extremities. This is also why the bacteria like armadillos. Despite their bulky shell, the creatures are some of the coolest, temperaturewise, of the animal kingdom.

Besides this particular health issue, the animals have other traits that set them apart. There's a joke down south that goes: *Why did the chicken cross the road? To taunt the armadillo.* The nine bands of bony plating typical of the southwestern species offer little defense against a Dodge Dakota hurtling along Texas's Highway 71. Armadillos don't do themselves any favors with their poor distance vision, their after-dark rambles, or their endearing-yet-suicidal habit of jumping high in the air when they feel threatened. This act may scare away Wile E. Coyote, but it offers no threat to the undercarriage of a three-ton SUV. Armadillos' hard-won reputation as speed bumps on legs is the main reason why they always get a full chapter in roadkill cookbooks.

In this regard, if eating a few bites of well-cooked armadillo carries theoretical risk, scraping a sun-baked bacteria tank off the side of the road for a cheap 'n' cheerful supper is another category of lunacy altogether. A recent study estimated that one out of every six armadillos living in Texas and Louisiana coastal marshes carries leprosy. According to an article in the *Southern Medical Journal,* "there have been several case reports of indigenously acquired leprosy in patients who reported extensive contact with armadillos, including trapping, curing, eating and wrestling armadillos."

Wrestling. Unfortunately the article does not elaborate on the practice of wrestling a nearsighted animal the size of a housecat. Thankfully, it is clear that leprosy is no longer the disfiguring curse it once was. If you happen to catch it, from an armadillo or some other source, the condition can be cured by a heavy round of antibiotics. Still, it's not something you want to go telling the neighbors . . .

Balut

Have you ever seen a hard-boiled-egg–eating contest, where bug-eyed participants stuff them down as fast as they can? Extreme? Think again. This spectacle is high tea at Harrod's compared to events at the festival of Santa Marta in Pateros, a town southeast of Manila in the Philippines. At this annual, weeklong celebration, the eggs' contents are not only hard-boiled but half-formed. In this, the hometown of the Filipino *balut* industry, contestants are eating seventeen-day-old mallard duck embryos that are plucked or sucked out of their shells.

Whenever a local food item is described as a

delicacy, take it as a warning that something grim will be coming soon to a place setting near you. Balut, the unofficial national street food of the Philippines, is indelicate in so many ways it's hard to list them in order, but here's a try:

1. If the bird is more mature than it's supposed to be, you can feel its little feathers with your tongue.

2. The smell has been described as "deliciously menstrual."

3. Embryonic guts dribble over your lips as you eat it, and the vendor may not have a napkin.

4. At the time of death the creature was drawing nutrition from its yolk sac, so its tubes, veins, and arteries are disproportionately huge.

5. It is sold late at night and early in the morning because it has a reputation as a potency enhancer. Your companions, having somehow talked you into trying it, will engage in clumsy wink-wink-nudge-nudges as you're trying to control your gag reflex.

Balut is sold from wicker baskets filled with sand or towels to keep the freshly boiled eggs warm. The traditional accompaniment is a bit of rock salt provided in a twist of paper; vinegar and chili sauce are also used as condiments. Filipinos insist that the finest balut is *balut sa puti*. This means "wrapped," the protoducklings enclosed in a white membrane—a kind of shroud that may allow the squeamish to avoid a good look. They say the seventeen-day-old-embryo is optimal for taste and texture; while in Vietnam they prefer an older, more textured balut, aged nineteen days.

If fate ever finds you on a Filipino street corner holding a warm egg in your hand, try to get a San Miguel in the other, for beer is the ideal accompaniment. Say a silent prayer to Santa Marta. Then go ahead and eat it with style:

1. Hold the egg vertically with the flatter side up. Tap the top with the back of a spoon or any other dull implement to get a crack going.

2. Pick away at the shell until you have a dime-sized opening in the top. Gently pierce the white inner membrane with a finger. Throw in some salt, tip the egg to your lips, and suck out the "broth" (amniotic fluid, best not to dwell on it, it will in fact taste pleasantly soupy).

3. Enlarge the hole so that you've taken away the top third of the shell. Remove more bits of membrane. At this point, you can go one of two ways. You can either bite at the balut and chip away at the shell, bite and chip, liberally using your salt, until you reach the inedible stone of hardened albumin, which you discard. Or—if you want to play to the crowd—you can ever-so-gently reach in and draw the entire embryo out, allowing it to dramatically unfurl before you eat it. Tastewise,

you will experience the equivalent of eggy duck custard, creamy, gooey, the bones barely gelled. With this accomplished, there's just a bit of "broth" left in the shell to swallow. During the dramatics, don't forget the San Mig in your other hand.

Who knows? You may love balut as much as the Filipinos do. And if not, look on the bright side. Even though you're out on the street and it's 2:00 a.m., balut—sold in nature's perfect package—is the most hygienic mouthful you could possibly find.

Bark

A random walk through the old-growth forests that still sprawl across stretches of Canada and the northern United States might afford a spooky sight. Pines, hemlocks, spruces, towering in the mist, and scarred in an unusual way. They're disfigured with regular, possibly rectangular lesions and semibands as much as three feet high and a half foot across. The outer bark has been ripped clean away, often with geometric precision, as though it were done with the help of a straight-edge.

What would do this kind of damage and why? Itchy-clawed bears with a freak sense of precision? The Blair Witch on a cross-country tour? Or, most demented of all, an environment artist hoping to scare up some grant money from the National Endowment for the Arts? The answer, of course, is none of the above. These excisions were left by indigenous peoples who found themselves craving the taste of bark.

People didn't hug trees a hundred years ago, but they did appreciate them in a way we moderns don't grasp. The Mohawks called a neighboring people "tree eaters," a name that stuck, and one that the Adirondacks seemed not to have resented. Sacagawea's tribe, the Shoshone, indulged in a taste for wood, as did the Rockies' Salish and Kootenai. The list of former bark-eaters is so lengthy that it's puzzling that the practice has, with the exception of the tropical bark cinnamon, gone so completely out of fashion today. By all accounts, bark tastes good. Sweet, reported many, and worthy enough to present to guests at important gatherings.

It's important to specify that the portion of the bark that was eaten was not the rough outer cortex, but what was revealed once this was stripped away. Hereunder lies the cambium, the cellular network that carries nutrients upward, most copiously in the spring. When the sap is rising, it does so within these channels. At this time of the year, the cambium is as thick as a stick of chewing gum, pliable, strippable, and rich with carbohydrates and minerals. An analysis of fresh hemlock has shown that starch and edible sugars contribute 26 percent of its food value, with a small protein content and substantial amounts of calcium and magnesium.

This was not a food to grow fat on, but, eaten fresh or dried into cakes, it added welcome variety to the woodland diet. According to the 1982 summation of archaeologist

Anne Eldridge, bark stripping was an important event in the calendar for many native peoples. Special tools were devised from antlers and bone to scrape, gouge, and peel away the tree's skin. These implements were often highly decorated and sought-after as items of trade. In Montana, according to Christine Whitacre's article in the newsletter of the Cooperative Ecosystems Studies Unit of the National Park Service, the Kootenai and Pend d'Oreille people began the procedure with a deep cut in the bark with an ax or stone knife. "A pole was thrust into the incision, and upward beneath the bark, serving as a lever to loosen the bark from the tree." These "culturally scarred" trees are drawing increasing interest as evidence of the lifestyles of the past. A survey undertaken in Glacier National Park identified fifty such trunks as of 2005.

In times of famine or survival in extremis, bark is still eaten, reinforcing its present-day reputation as a food of last resort. Purely voluntary bark eating is practically unknown. Cambium is impossible to come by unless you have a stand of sweet-sapped trees on your property. Would-be bark strippers are well advised to get a solid identification of the tree in question to ensure that the cambium is edible, and to never, ever cut a ring all the way around the tree, because this will cut off its circulation and kill it. The taste can be experienced far more easily in the balsam and cedar jellies sold by internet purveyors, or in the balsam-shoot sorbet recipe provided by Anita Stewart in her *Flavours of Canada* cookbook. Granted, they are a few steps removed from the raw material favored by the Adirondacks, but the spirit of the forest lives within them.

Barnacle

If you're having a meal in a seaside restaurant in Spain or Portugal and adventurously order *percebes*, sight unseen, you may be perplexed by the creature that appears on the dish. You won't be the first. Back in the eleventh century, wise minds took a look at its black, inch-long neck and tulip-shaped head and decided it was an infantile goose that would eventually sprout feathers and blast out of the sea. Centuries later, the young Charles Darwin investigated more closely and wound up writing a four-volume natural history on the animal, by then definitively classified as a barnacle, but retaining the name "gooseneck." Today, food writers are claiming that gooseneck barnacles are the next big thing, poised to become stars on high-end restaurant menus.

At a biological level, these are prehistoric creatures with better staying power than dinosaurs. They live in massive colonies along the rocky coastlines of Spain, Portugal, Morocco, and the west coast of the United States and Canada. While individually the animals compete neck and neck for food and shelf space, their wave-tossed colonies also work as a unit to trap plankton-rich seawater. This helps prolong mealtime and facilitates reproduction. The creatures are hermaphroditic, having both male and female sexual organs, but prefer to be fertilized by whatever barnacle happens to be next door.

The creatures have a distinct flair for bondage, clinging to the rocks with a unique cement that is the envy of materials chemists. When a free-floating juvenile barnacle has found a place to lodge, it secretes the glue from special glands located in its head. Once the glue hardens, a dime-sized, microthin patch can support up to seven thousand pounds at temperatures over 300°F. Obviously the cement is waterproof; it's also impervious to strong acids, alkalis, and organic solvents. If man can ever learn to synthesize this adhesive, it will revolutionize the way bones are set, among countless other possibilities. For now, though, it's still the barnacle's trade secret.

The brave men who harvest the goosenecks are less enthusiastic about the cement's bonding power. Dislodging barnacles from rocks is still done much as it has been for centuries. A crew of souls in high-traction shoes clamber over craggy surge channels and hang on for their lives if a particularly massive wave comes crashing in. Since the creatures live in the intertidal zone—the few feet of vertical space that is exposed between low tide and high—harvesting can only take place for a few hours to either side of a daylit low tide. Careful not to turn their backs on the sea, the harvesters use a metal pry implement attached to a long wooden pole to chip the animals from their strongholds.

It is dangerous work. Speaking to the *International Herald Tribune*, José Pose, director of the Marine Rescue Coordinating Center in Aguino, Spain, said, "Calls about barnacle fishermen are the worst . . . usually the best we can do is retrieve the corpse." Given the consequences of bad decision-making, harvesters develop a whole-body attunement to conditions and climate. Like firefighting and giant-slalom skiing, this is a job where losing a sense of the environment and one's exact position within it, even for a moment, can mean the difference between life and death.

The barnacle poses a far more pleasant challenge to the first-time diner. When the percebes arrive from their boiling bath of seawater, you grasp one by the stalk and bite a puncture into the skin, aware of the potential jet of orange liquid that may be its last line of defense. Suck this juice clean; then, placing the fingers to either side of the incision, peel away the skin on the stalk to reveal the rubbery neck, whose flesh has a mussel-like flavor and texture. A crisp white wine is an excellent accompaniment to the dish. As you relax into your meal, lift a glass to the harvesters who wrested this prehistoric delicacy to your table.

Bat

Bat soup used to be big on the Pacific island of Guam, where it was a traditional feast dish for the native Chamorro people. But after World War II, overhunting and other environmental pressures took a massive toll and the bats' numbers dwindled. Still hankering for their favorite festival dish, the Chamorro turned to neighboring islands to fill the pots, and between 1975 and 1988, they imported over two hundred thousand bats from elsewhere in the Pacific. It all proved too much for the Mariana fruit bat and its diminutive relative, the little Mariana fruit bat. Nearing extinction all over the region, the animals finally found sanctuary under international treaty and protected status granted by the U.S. government. But this is not the story of a helpless animal being eaten to near extinction, then getting a reprieve once the feds rode to the rescue. Or not only. Because on the island of Guam, the bat managed to get in blows of its own. Experts have only recently discovered that eating native bat soup packed a penalty that makes federal sanctions look trifling.

Preparing bat soup Chamorro-style was straightforward. You'd catch a Mariana fruit bat (also known as a flying fox due to its doggy appearance), immerse it whole in a pot of boiling milk, and cook it for a couple hours. Eating was straightforward too, because there was no complicated decision-making about which parts to eat and which parts to discard. You ate everything but the bones, including the fur, guts, and wings. Little gone to waste, all well and good, except that the fruit bat's own diet exposed you to a mind-warping peril.

The fruit bats on Guam are especially fond of the seeds of the local cycad plants, which happen to contain a potent neurotoxin. When people tucked into a home-grown bat at wedding feasts, as they did up until the 1970s, they got a double hit of cycad toxin: not only the chemical residue in the bat's tissues, but also the partially digested pieces of seed still in the animal's intestines. Which explains why, up until the 1970s, the number-one killer of adult Chamorro people was an otherwise rare disease called ALS-PDC (for short), which tragically causes dementia, tremors, and paralysis. Since the offending plant doesn't grow on other islands, the incidence of the disease let up dramatically once the bats began to be imported from other parts.

Since these particular toxic seeds aren't found outside of Guam, the bold culinary adventurer might decide it's safe to sample bat in places like Palau, a Micronesian island midway between Guam and Borneo, where the animal is also served in soup. Or perhaps in Cambodia, where Phnom Penh restaurants display the creatures in front-of-the-house cages before dishing them up curried or raw. Here the bold culinary adventurer would be quite wrong, especially if he or she has any kind of gum trouble.

Cycad toxins are but one of the curses a flying fox can cast against hungry humans. We would all do well to be very, very afraid of a plate of undercooked bat. In 2002, a team of U.S. scientists set out to identify up-and-coming viruses in Southeast Asia. In Cambodia, they took blood specimens from restaurant fruit bats. Of ninety-six animals tested, eleven showed evidence of infection with the newly discovered Nipah virus, which, according to the World Health Organization, causes "inflammation of the brain (encephalitis), with drowsiness, disorientation, convulsions, and coma. Fifty percent of the clinically apparent cases die."

The vampire bat may have the worst reputation in the order Chiroptera, but the most dangerous may in fact be the gentle, vegetarian, relatively handsome fruit bat. Especially if you find yourself wandering by night with a taste for its blood.

Bee Brood

Experienced raiders use smoke and great caution to drive a swarm of enraged honeybees from a wild hive. But not all of the hive's occupants fly away. Some can't. Wingless and dependent in the cells of the comb are the abandoned juveniles. They provide small blasts of protein amid the carbohydrate goodness that is honey. In the Congo, according to G. Parent, F. Malaisse, and C. Verstraeten (translated by Gene DeFoliart and presented in DeFoliart's online book, *The Human Use of Insects as a Food Resource*), "The villagers are very fond of larvae, thus they generally cannot resist the pleasure of tasting some by chewing the operculated [sealed] cell, the wax then being spit out again."

"Bee brood" is shorthand for the larval and pupal residents of the lower sections of a comb complex—in effect, the hive's nursery level. The individual pupae and larvae are clumped together by microthin layers of wax. When a fresh comb is broken apart you see the larvae wiggling, pathetic hungry spirals in search of the worker bees, which in better times were their caretakers.

In parts of the world a larva-stuffed comb is so prized that it is sold by the chunk in local markets. Westerners who equate hives solely with honey tend to be more squeamish about its white and squirmy occupants. But as a food, raw bee brood isn't entirely as bad as it looks. The larvae are extremely bland in flavor. The most disconcerting thing about them is their tendency to burst with a splat between the teeth, yielding a freaky amount of juice for such a small package. Also less than delightful is the chew-resistant quality of the skin, which causes it to gum up in the molars' crevices (much like the skin of defrosted frozen blueberries). Between the larval and pupal skin and the beeswax, which also sticks, your teeth tend to pack tight pretty quickly.

At the riotously beguiling jungle market near Lampang, in northern Thailand, representatives of the northern hill tribes sell local foods and wares. There you'll find a more elaborate preparation of honeybee brood. Smoking atop small braziers at the hive-product stalls are palm-sized clumps of brood packed into large green banana leaves, sealed with a toothpick, and grilled over hot coals. As the leaf chars black, the food within steams. Unwrapping the package reveals a not-terribly-appetizing white-gray mass. In this case, looks are deceiving: cooking definitely improves this food's appeal. The steaming concentrates the sweetness of the honey-fed larvae and makes their texture denser and more palatable. It also breaks down the elastic in the skin and melts off most of the wax. Prepared in this way, bee brood tastes much like field-fresh corn on the cob.

Toothpicks are provided on the market tables (vendors here sell lots of things that will stick in the teeth). Also, in case you were wondering, when you're eating bee brood (fresh or cooked), it's acceptable to discreetly spit out inedible bits on your paper plate.

Betel Nut

You know you're in betel territory when the gobs you see on the sidewalk aren't the dull pink or gray patties of spent chewing gum but a glistening, lurid red, the telltale color of spit tinged with *Areca catechu*. And spit they do, the chewers of betel, for the nut's active ingredients, the alkaloids arecaine and arecoline, increase saliva flow to flood level. Betel addicts think of this as part of the fun. If a hard-core chewer can't get outside during office hours, the soft-drink can he's using as a spittoon is in danger of spilling over onto his paperwork.

Crimson smiles have been a fixture in southern Asia and the Pacific region for over two thousand years. Betel culture is still deeply embedded. In Taiwan, betel shops lure business with live window dressing: pretty girls selling the orange-green nuts and the paraphernalia that goes with them. These "betel beauties" also operate from trucks and street stalls on busy corners, throwing themselves into their work with such sparkling enthusiasm and scantiness of dress that the Taipei police, citing a long list of traffic accidents, had a crackdown in September 2004, insisting the girls cover up and tone down the act.

In some countries, like Guam, the quartered nut of the betel palm is typically chewed au naturel. Elsewhere you find elaborations and embellishments. The basic upgrade is known as the betel quid. It consists of chopped or grated nut; a pinch of lime (calcium oxide, made from baked seashells or coral), which amplifies the hit of the nut's mildly psychoactive alkaloids; and a wrapper made of the biting, aromatic leaf of the betel pepper plant, which is related to the nut only by longstanding association. Once the packet is tucked into the cheek, it is chewed and sucked and lolled around until the drooly, spicy savor of the fibrous mass is tapped out, anywhere from minutes to hours later. By then the effects have kicked in: a mild, buzzy euphoria accompanied by raised heart rate and skin temperature, and the aforementioned crimson spit gush. Incorporating as it does minute particles of chewed betel nut, an expectoration leaves a sink looking like it's been party to a bad household accident.

Thanks to commercial farming of the betel palm and the introduction of ready-to-use blends, betel use is on the rise. There are an estimated several hundred million users in the world, ranging from children as young as five to the elderly. Immigrants have brought betel culture to their new lands, with nuts and blends available in ethnic food stores and on the internet. Dried betel travels well and is as habit-forming as fresh betel. Indian mixtures called *paan masala* incorporate powdered betel and spices like nutmeg, cardamom, cloves, and sweeteners, and are sold preblended in individual sachets or tins. *Gupta*, a blend that includes tobacco, lends an additional jolt from nicotine.

Chewers insist that betel has health benefits, like cavity prevention and worm expulsion. But the substance is universally recognized to be addictive, with potential side effects including diarrhea, nausea, vomiting, stomach cramps, teeth permanently stained red or black, urinary incontinence, seizures, and heart attacks. It's also been implicated by the International Agency for Research on Cancer as a cancer-causing agent. Before a cancer sets in, the chewer may experience a condition called oral submucous fibrosis, which causes the skin inside the cheeks to turn so leathery that it's impossible to close the mouth (not a pretty picture if a user persists in the betel habit; now the spit can only dribble vampirically out). Oral cancers are keeping pace with increased betel consumption: the World Health Organization reports that incidence of male oral cancer in betel regions of Asia well outstrips its occurrence elsewhere.

Betel is a source of sustenance, but not for its meager calories. It is a mood-management tool that actually works to dampen the appetite. So it's little wonder that despite the warnings of health authorities, it is a much-loved indulgence where hard work, tedium, and a monotonous diet are standard factors of daily life.

Big-ass Ant

☹ ↗

"Whoa. Those are some big-ass ants."

This isn't just an idle comment in the state of San-tander, Colombia. *Hormigas culonas*—more politely trans-lated as "big-bottomed ants"—are what locals call members of the leaf-cutting *Atta* species. While these creatures can defoliate an orange grove practically overnight, they atone for this sin by serving as a much-loved snack. The affection people have for the insects is evident in this superbly non-PC joke told by writer Felix Villabona Ordonez:

A well-dressed and haughty older lady makes her way through the market. She stops at a vendor displaying basketfuls of big-ass ants.

"How much do they cost?" she asks in a rushed, impatient way.

"Fifteen pesos a pound, madam."

"Fifteen pesos! Impossible. A little thing like that, so expen-sive. You've got to be kidding." Hoping to get a bargain, she tries to negotiate. "OK, my good man, how about this. You keep their heads. Does that get me a better price?"

The seller looks at her stunned. Then he replies, in a philo-sophical way: "Please forgive my honesty, madam, but here in

Santander, we value the ant the same way we value our women. It's the bottom, not the top, that counts."

Ah, the smell of roasted ants in the morning. Twice a year, the smoke wafts over the Santander villages of Barichara, Guane, Mesa de los Santos, and others. For residents, it signifies two things: a hot appetizer and—according to a thousand years of local legend—even hotter sex. For the big-asses aren't any old ants scraped up off the forest floor. These are virgin queens, swept from the air en route to (or from) their mating trysts. The sexual fulfillment sought by the insects is thought to imbue them with strong aphrodisiac powers. The ants are likewise thought to increase fertility, and are served by the bowlful during marriage ceremonies.

The ant's hindquarters are so very big, about the size of a pea, because they hold a potential colony of up to two million individuals. During clear patches in the rainy periods in April and October, the virgin queens swarm from their birth nests, intent on mating and forming colonies of their own. They've doused themselves with pheromones to look shiny and smell nice. Unlike their human counterparts in similar circumstances, they are blissfully unconcerned about the size of their butts.

By the thousands they take high into the air in a spiral pattern, their beating wings audible a hundred meters away. During the next two to three minutes they experience their first and last acts of love with incoming males, who, after flying over to perform their sole earthly duty, drop dead. The queens, thus initiated into the two-hundred-meter-high club, drift to a landing, rip off their wings, find a suitable spot, and for the next fifteen days, all on their own, dig, laying the foundations for a new colony that may eventually stretch the length of a city block.

Unless they're interrupted midair by the swinging basket of a Santander harvester. During the few weeks of big-ass ant season, a harvester can earn the equivalent of a year's wages. If the creatures are to be cooked on the spot, they are brought to a central roasting tent and stirred in a handful of salt and oil in a mud pot over an open fire (their abdomens toasting until they blow open like popcorn). Some ants are held aside for live shipment to Santander's capital, Bucaramanga, where they're cooked fresh at special stands and sold on street corners and at the airport for about two dollars per hundred-gram bag. Occasionally, bagfuls also make their way to Colombia's capital, Bogotá, but anyone hoping to find them for sale in movie theaters (a frequently repeated travel-guide assertion) is liable to be disappointed. According to Colombian Alejandro Gomez, the ants have a crispy texture and a peanutty taste that grows on you, making it hard to stop once you get started. "They're a fun item to eat," he says, "especially if you wash them down with a bit of Colombian *aguardiente* [fire water]."

Unless you're traveling to the Santander region during ant-swarming season, these animals can be tricky to find. In Japan they're available in cans. Recently, they've also been airshipped out of Colombia by an internet purveyor of exotic foods, selling to Europe and America. So they are slowly making their way into the wider world. If they catch on, in addition to a hot snack and hotter sex in the villages of Santander, the big-ass will signify cold cash.

Bird's Nest Soup

☹ ↗ 🐾

Some diners never complain to their waiter, for fear of getting some spit in their soup. Then there are those who pay handsomely for it. These people congregate in upscale Chinese restaurants, where the saliva in question comes not from the kitchen staff, but from a little bird known as the cave swiftlet.

In China and in Chinese communities around the world, bird's nest soup is revered for its health benefits. Among its alleged properties are the ability to rejuvenate cells, restore ailing lungs, clear the skin, and shore up "youthful vigor." Whether the soup has any actual benefits boils down to whether you align with traditional Chinese medicine or orthodox science. The scientist will say that the long preparation and cooking process leaches away most of the nest's nutritional value. But try telling that to a true believer. Bird's nest soup lovers believe any food so very pricey while at the same time so bereft of innate flavor has *got* to work, otherwise why bother eating it at all?

The mucilaginous broth has its beginnings in the tropical coastlands of Malaysia, Vietnam, Thailand, and elsewhere in Southeast Asia. Here live the various species of cave swiftlets, three-to-five-inch-long, extremely fastflying birds whose unusual toe configuration hinders their

ability to roost on branches. Instead, they fashion A-cup-sized nests that cantilever off the upper reaches of sea cliffs or the walls of limestone caves.

Nest construction begins when a swiftlet, feeling the yearly urge to settle down and raise a family, gorges on seaweed, the raw material behind the bricks and mortar. Salivary glands under the tongue enlarge, the better to secrete sticky ropes of mucus that the bird—at this point an avian glue gun—sculpts into a bracket against the cave or cliff wall. Within minutes, the saliva hardens. Buttressed by twigs and other bits and pieces, the nest is eventually big enough to support the bird and two eggs.

You'd think the out-of-the-way location would keep nests safe from predators. And it does, with one major exception. Somehow, the nests became a table item during the Tang dynasty, after sailors brought them back to China as a special treat for the emperor and his family. A costly delicacy they have been ever since, their harvest zealously overseen by large-scale distributors.

Ideally, the eggs hatch and the baby birds are airworthy before the home is snapped clear of its cliffside moorings. But in the real world, the prices that the nests command (anywhere from $2,000 to $5,000 a kilo, amounting to about 120 nests) means haste often wins out over scrupulous inspection for occupants. As a result, wild swiftlet populations are in decline in many regions of Asia.

While taking an active nest is deplorable for humane and ecological reasons, it is hard to peg the harvesters as villians, given the conditions they work under. How many of us would do better, climbing a lashed-together rattan scaffolding two hundred feet up a cave wall, clutching a sharpened bamboo dislodging pole, the air pitch-dark, unbearably humid, thick with bugs and the ammoniac reek of guano, and cut through with richoceting, echolocating birds and bats? It's a terrible job, and like so many of its kind, it is one you are condemned to by birth, since the expertise passes from fathers to sons.

It's possible to get a cleaned-up glimpse into the lives of nest makers and nest takers at the Niah Caves of Niah National Park in Borneo. In the Great Cave you can see (but not test) the scaffolding, walk on the guano trench that yielded the remains of the Java Man, and witness the commute known as "the changing of the guard," where the cave swiftlets sail back to their nests past streams of bats headed out for the night.

Elsewhere in cave swiftlet territory, the welcome will be much less friendly. Typically, guards patrol cave mouths with automatic weapons, protecting the interests of powerful concession holders thousands of miles away. Harvesting rights are multiyear, multimillion-dollar deals arranged with national governments and ruthlessly enforced against poachers. This is hardball: unarmed fishermen have been shot dead after accidentally beaching in swiftlet territory, and local excursion operators pay extortionate fees to avoid the hazard of scope-assisted leaks springing in their kayaks.

After the nests are harvested, shipments reach a processing center and the long job of cleanup begins. This is a time-consuming task that even the most prep-happy chef is willing to leave to professionals. First, the nests are soaked to loosen the cemented strands. Then feathers, twigs, and other big pieces of what-have-you are carefully extracted. Take a walk down Wing Lok Street in Hong Kong and you'll see ladies behind counters in the bird's nest specialty shops patiently, painstakingly, and at lightning speed picking matter out of the nests with large metal tweezers. Eventually the nests are as clean as the women can get them, and there is a small heap of feathers, poop, and other matter on the tray below. With another round of soaking, smaller contaminants like dead lice and seaweed fragments float away. Farther back in the shop, you might see a woman drying a trayful of just-boiled pure white bird's nests—the highest grade—with a blow-dryer. All this grooming results in nests that are touching in their delicacy. In them you see the sheer biological determination—of bird and man—that converted bits of seaweed on a South Pacific beach into a brightly packaged luxury in a gourmet food store.

Despite all the effort involved in its trip to the table, bird's nest soup is not a major experience in terms of flavor. Simmering for hours in stock with bits of meat certainly helps lend it some personality. More aggressively, rock sugar may be added to make the popular sweet version of the soup. In both versions the strands taste like ultrathin, underdone rice noodles. Not that its many fans care. They're convinced by the health claims, or they enjoy the luxury of a pricey treat, or they have some other arcane rationale for eating it, like this one, recently posted on a food website: "It's the closest you'll ever get to making out with a swallow."

There is good news on the swiftlet survival front. Recognizing a profit center when they see one, communities around Southeast Asia are encouraging the birds to nest in abandoned buildings, luring them with prerecorded swiftlet songs and bird chatter to check out the new model homes. It's a new phase in a very old relationship—one that hopefully will ensure a healthy old age for the cave swiftlet as a species.

Blubber

In *Some Aspects of Sea Ice Subsistence in Point Hope, Alaska,* Tom Lowenstein describes the fearsome, ancestral rigor that Inupiat boatmen bring to a whale hunt:

It is the discipline of the operation which continues. . . . Complaining about the cold—except to joke about it—is frowned upon and those members who sleep "too much" may be teased by those stronger-willed and more experienced crew members who are set-

ting the style of the "sitting" with an example of vigilance and toughness. And when a whale rises, and the umiaq *is launched, it is unthinkable that any man should relax for a moment . . .*

Today, the watercraft that pursue the sounding mammal are as likely to be outboard-powered aluminum Formula Vees as they are sealskin *umiaqs* powered by plunging oars, but the ethos of the hunt has remained substantially the same over the centuries. A six-ton bowhead whale brought to shore provides considerable bounty in the isolated regions of the Arctic.

For the people who live in this region, simply keeping warm in the subzero temperatures comes at a massive metabolic cost: experiments on polar explorers have shown that active individuals can burn up to three thousand calories a day solely to maintain body temperature — never mind the added exertions of exercise and other metabolic functions. The fat-rich tissues of whale, seal, and walrus provide the caloric energy necessary for survival, as well as vital nutrients. Whale oil, for example, is rich in vitamin C, explaining why native Arctic peoples escaped scurvy in a place where fresh fruit was scarce.

When a catch is brought in, a village rejoices, as described by Lowenstein:

As the whale is towed to a suitable spot . . . the men raise their voices in the "joy shout" (qatchaq), a ringing syllable of dance-cry (Ui! ui!) which is pressed from the throat on an abrupt exhalation, like a walrus barking . . . in the village, the church bell rings — a mysterious but happy awakening if it should occur in the small hours of the weekday . . . women too old to make the journey come out of the houses and dance in the open.

Butchering an animal that is as long as a stretch limo is a villagewide enterprise that can take several days. First, one or several forklifts bring the creature to the designated processing area. The dismemberment begins with the flukes cut from the tail—the initial cut typically made by the captain who first weakened the animal by harpoon or rifle. Then large strips of the gunmetal-gray skin and the attached layer of tawny-pink, fatty blubber (*maktak* or *muktuk* or *maktaaq*) are sectioned off with a cutting tool that resembles a giant wooden-handled scalpel. A portion of the flesh is rendered on the spot to release oil, which itself is an important foodstuff. Then the oil and man-sized chunks of blubber, meat, and viscera are apportioned among the village members, who store it in their household freezer (often a purpose-made hole underground) for the months ahead. By butchering's end, the underlying snow is stained Day-Glo pink. The animal's carcass and head—considered the seat of its soul—are tipped back into the water with the shouted request to "come back next year."

If eaten fresh, whale blubber has a nutty, salty taste some people say is like almonds, and a pliable, resilient texture. Its fishy flavor intensifies when it is preserved, as described in this old Kwakiutl recipe translated by Bruce Hallman:

Take cedar bark, and split it into long strips. Poke holes in the middle of the boiled pieces of whale blubber, and thread them onto the long strips of bark . . . dry these strips in the smoky rafters of your house for at least a month. . . . When you want to eat some, take it down from the rafters and boil it in a kettle until tender. This takes a lot of boiling. Be sure to eat it hot, because when it is cold, it is really tough.

It's important to note that "really tough" for iron-jawed Inuits means close to inedible for anyone else. Even a piece of fresh blubber will keep your mouth busy for quite a long time — which is why Inuit mothers often give babies a piece as a pacifier. Those in the know say this: the longer you chew, the better it tastes. If it happens to be winter in the Arctic Circle, you've got a long night ahead of you to find out.

Bone Marrow

Faced with a heap of roasted marrow bones, people tend to take one of two stands. Some find this food categorically gross, from the gelatinous wiggly marrow tissue to the cross-sectioned femurs to the metal instrument used to extract it. For others, this is what heaven looks like, sliced. They eat the marrow with a greedy passion, wistfully setting down the bones only when every last gobbet has been scraped out.

Not so long ago, we were all marrow lovers by default, because this is the ultimate survival food. Rich, soft, and fatty, the wellspring of the body's blood cells, it fills the central channels of the long bones, most rewardingly of large grazers like cattle and deer. Since the substance slips right down the throat, it is ideal for the very young, the very old, the sick, and the dentally handicapped. Marrow is also superb nutritionally. In our current mode of overconsumption we pay lip service to good nutrition. When "hunter" and "gatherer" were the only occupations on the employment questionnaire, the food pyramid wasn't just a guideline but a life-and-death matter. Fat was a critical element.

Communities that depended on the forest, field, and stream for food were particularly fat-hungry in the late winter and early spring, when the stored fat of their prey was at its lowest. If the muscle meat of deer, rabbits, buffalo, and other quarry becomes too lean, eating too much of it can actually sicken—a syndrome some Native Americans called "rabbit poisoning." But hunters knew that even in the most barren times of the year, health-giving fat remained deep in the animals' bones. Marrow tasted meaty and greasy and voluptuous, and it satisfied the appetite much longer than a ropy filet mignon.

If one's troubles stemmed from overindulgence, marrow also came to the rescue. In Kenneth Roberts's classic 1938 novel of exploration, *Northwest Passage*, the critically wounded explorer McNott explains: "I dunno nothing better for a delicate stomach than marrow, whether it's boiled or roasted. It's sweet and it melts in your mouth, so you don't have to chew it. A feller that's suffering from too much rum, so he can't touch no ordinary vittles without wishing he was dead, he can eat marrow. It just kind of trickles all through him, and soothes him when he needs it most."

Marrow does have a shortcoming. Like a princess in a tower, it can be hard to get out. Eons ago, entire families of mammals evolved to do just that: they were natural-born bone crushers, sporting large teeth, thick lower jaws, and reinforced skulls. The hyena is one of the few surviving examples. Man, with his more delicate facial structure, devised primitive tools to help: splitters, smashers, and reamers made of stone. Archaeologists routinely find the heaped remains of marrow-extraction works, more evidence of the importance of the substance in the ancient diet.

By the eighteenth century in England, the European continent, and America, sets of marrow picks, scoops, and spoons made of sterling silver, engraved with the owners' initials in elaborate script, were essential components of the *batterie de cuisine* in every upper-class household. Nowadays they sell in antique shops and on eBay, sought after more as fine collectibles than as working items.

A handsome stainless-steel marrow pick can be yours, for a little while, if you order the roasted marrow bones at St. John in London. The restaurant's founder, Fergus Henderson, follows the philosophy that "there is a set of delights, textural and flavoursome, which lie beyond the fillet." He has single-handedly resuscitated marrow bones as a stand-alone dish in fine restaurants. "It's the sensuality," he says, when asked why he serves veal bones in preference to those of an older animal. "They feel right in the hand."

And so they do, a warm, slender, polished cylinder in one hand and the pick in the other, working out the marrow, spreading it on thick-sliced sourdough toast, and sprinkling it with crunchy rock salt. Tasting this refined reiteration of a primal food, you can imagine how the ancestors must have felt as marrow goodness seeped into their own bones.

Boodog

The most extreme thing about boodog, one of the great national dishes of Mongolia, is not that its main ingredient is frequently marmot, a groundhog-sized mountain rodent.

It is not that marmots are still among the most notorious carriers of bubonic plague, the cause of the Black Death, killer of two hundred million people in fourteenth-century Europe, the worst toll from any disease ever. In the marmot, the bacteria live in the animal's bloodstream or in the guts of fleas residing in the animal's pelt.

It is not that the hunters, well aware of the marmots' health issues, go ahead and shoot them anyway (sparing only those that are blatantly frothing and reeling around).

It is not that the animals, once shot, are brought back to the encampment, slit through the throat, and disemboweled organ by organ, by hand.

It is not that the marmots are then salted and stuffed with specially selected red-hot rocks that are manipulated with metal fireplace tongs, so that the meat will begin to cook from the inside out.

The most extreme thing about boodog is that the cooking process is finished from the outside in, with a blowtorch, whereby the hair is singed off and the skin roasted to a crackling brown.

To clarify: this is no palm-sized culinary blowtorch from the Williams-Sonoma catalog sold with four porcelain ramekins and detailed instructions on how to finish crème brûlée with a lacy caramelized sugar crust.

No, there are no antiflare or safety-lock features on this baby. If it's not an actual flamethrower, mislaid on training maneuvers by the Mongolian army, it's probably an antique Primus brass-bottom job, fired on kerosene. Special features include a rusty valve, choking fumes, and flares galore. It's all part of the fun of cooking boodog, which, once done to a turn, is cooled a bit, then held over a plastic bucket. The greasy cooking rocks are pulled out (to be passed by hand from diner to diner as a traditional gesture of good fellowship). Then the beast itself is cut apart with one's own or a communal knife and eaten with the hands. According to Deb McCown, a journalist who has lived in Mongolia, "marmot is said to taste like horsemeat, which isn't bad, but is extremely tough . . . the greasiest, fattiest, densest meats (horse and marmot) are called 'hot' meats and are considered healthiest by Mongolians—essentially the opposite of what a cardiologist would tell you, but suited the frigid climate where the more calories the better."

It is probably completely unnecessary to point out that cooking boodog—at least in the final, blue-flame stage—is man's work. If you are ever given the honor of holding the blowtorch, it's a good idea to stand as far back from the animal as possible. Hot fleas will jump.

Botfly Larvae

In times past, snacks were hard to come by on the barren tundra of the Arctic Circle. Vending machines were non-existent, fresh berries were seasonal, and game hunting meant a full day's work. So reindeer herders watching over their livestock had limited options. Luckily, little morsels just bursting with goodness were found right on the backs of the reindeer—not in saddlebags or packs, but literally in the skin of the animals. Botfly larvae are para-sites that burrow in a pronounced lump underneath the pelt of their host. It is possible for a skilled larva extractor to coax them out whole via their airholes. The technique is not unlike self-treatment of a mature pimple, except the herder ate what came out.

For this, the reindeer was profoundly grateful, for the pest had been gnawing its flesh all winter long. The tor-ment began months earlier, in the spring, when adult war-ble flies hatched from their casings and immediately began feeling frisky. After successfully mating, the female of the species flew off looking for a shapely reindeer leg, upon which she deposited her eggs. Since the reindeer detest playing Winnebago for warble fly larvae, they responded by stamping, stampeding, and generally running amok. In the end, the flies got their way, and within a few days after the eggs were laid, tiny larvae emerged and burrowed under the reindeer's skin. Then, in an incredible feat of pitch-dark navigation, they tunneled their way to the top of the animal's back, walled themselves off within cysts, bit an airhole through the skin, and hunkered down, nibbling away, until they emerged, yellowish white, ribbed, and about 2.5 centimeters long, the following spring. The larvae then dropped to the earth, where they would burrow, pupate, and hatch as mature flies, starting the cycle anew.

Unless a hungry herder extracted them first. One observer, writing in 1918, reported that "the Eskimos pick out the grubs from the hides in the spring and eat them like cherries." Another account explains that "they are always eaten raw and alive out of the skin and are said by those who like them to be as fine as gooseberries."

These days, botfly larvae remain largely unmolested, though now and then an old-timer with a taste for the traditional might start feeling for lumps on Donder's back. According to Zona Spray Starks, an expert on Arctic cuisine, botfly larvae are still eaten, though they are not as sought after as they were in the old days. Says Starks, "People consider them a delicacy, much like many cultures that enjoy a feast of bugs."

Reindeer aren't the only animals that endure suffering by this pest. There is extensive medical documentation of human infestation with botfly larvae. If you've recently visited the tropics and find yourself nursing a suspicious swelling with a porelike hole at its center, a visit to a specialist may be in order. A doctor will have the instruments necessary for safe, sterile, and complete removal. The other option is, of course, a reindeer herder with a taste for the old ways, but these days they're getting harder and harder to find.

Calf's Head

Vegetarians agree on the principle of not eating anything that has a face. Many more of us agree on the principle of not eating anything that *is* a face. Still, *tête de veau*—calf's head—remains a popular dish in old-school restaurants in France.

Calf's head is an unforgiving test of the chef's abilities and, if they fall short, the diner's ability to get through the meal. Elizabeth David, the great English cookery writer and champion of French cuisine, had this to say about the dish: "When it is served really tender and hot and you get a comparatively lean piece and the vinaigrette sauce has been well mixed, then it is quite good. More often, it is repellent." In *A Cook's Tour*, Anthony Bourdain elaborates: "Usually (the way I make it anyway) it's a slice of rolled-up boneless calf's face, peeled right off the skull, tied up—with a stuffing of sweetbreads—and served boiled in a little broth, a few nicely shaped root vegetables and a slice of tongue. It's an acquired taste, or more accurately, an acquired texture: the translucent fat, the blue calf's skin, and the bits of cheek and thymus gland take some getting past before you can actually enjoy the flavor."

The last thing you want to do, if you're feeling positive about the tastes and textures of calf's head, is to pop into the kitchen to check out the preparation. Even the redoubtable Elizabeth David warns that "to cook it at home is a scarifying process." If you insist, she provides a recipe. After steeping the head overnight, and then boiling it for ten minutes, you must "wipe off any scum that is sticking to the animal's skin." David must have missed Lydia Child's tip in the 1829 *American Frugal Housewife*: "It is better to leave the windpipe on, for if it hangs out of the pot while the head is cooking, all the froth will escape through it."

Once the head is parboiled the really gruesome work begins, as depicted in the morgueworthy step-by-step photographs on the website Chefsimon.com. Chef Simon's French captions mince no words: "Frankly, this is going to get ugly." As for the pictures, they need no translation. We see the fatal bolt-hole in the animal's shaven pate. The flayed skin laid out to either side of the head ("like Jar-Jar or Dumbo"). The lolling tongue. The bone saw through the back of the skull ("Don't cut too far or you'll wind up with a lobotomy"). The scooping out of brains ("Now we're in Hannibal territory").

If this, the classic deboned and rolled preparation, seems like too much fuss, there is an alternative: calf's head sawn in half, cooked, and served *comme ça* on a platter. When the meat is still attached to the skull, carving requires a deft hand. Mrs. Beeton—another redoubtable British cook whose 1861 *Book of Household Management* remains a classic—offers these tips:

This is not altogether the most easy-looking dish to cut when it is put before a carver for the first time; there is not much real difficulty in the operation, however, when the head has been attentively examined, and, after the manner of the phrenologist, you get to know its bumps, good and bad. . . . The eye, and the flesh round, are favourite morsels with many, and should be given to those at the table who are known to be the greatest connoisseurs. The jawbone being removed, there will then be found some nice lean; and the palate, which is reckoned by some a tit-bit, lies under the head. On a separate dish there is always served the tongue and brains, and each guest should be asked to take some of these.

As any good guest would, for fear of losing face.

Casu Marzu

In the mountainous interior of Sardinia, a large island located off the west coast of Italy, the sloping meadows are covered with sheep, whose rich, herb-flavored milk is made into one of the island's major exports, pecorino cheese. From the highly regarded spicy-sharp *fiore Sardo* (flower of Sardinia) to fluffy ricottas to pecorino-Romano that is grated in the best restaurants around the world, the range of flavors, textures, and appearances is remarkable. Still, if cheese happens to be a primary source of nourishment for three meals a day—as it is for many shepherd families—it's understandable why they might hanker for *something extra*, some random factor that pushes the cheese into a new flavor realm.

Which can be the only possible explanation for the existence of *casu marzu*, also known as *casu mode* or *formaggio marcio*. All of which mean "rotten cheese." And that is exactly what it is: stinking, running, tongue-burning stuff, traditionally eaten at the end of a meal, a soft glob wrapped in *pane carasau*, Sardinian bread, and washed down with the local red wine.

Eating it is a bonding ritual of Sardinian manhood. Sharing it is a key part of the experience. And not just with the friends and family gathered around the table. Others are enjoying the cheese at the same time: the host of tiny maggots that riddles the stuff. A really righteous hunk of casu marzu is teeming with worms: pale, nearly transparent creatures whose own digestive enzymes join forces with the cheese's self-started decomposition to create a festival of rot.

If left alone with their formaggio, the gorged larvae would eventually climb out and find a dark, quiet place to dissolve within their pupae, then turn into grown-up flies. This is as nature intended for *Piophila casei*, or cheese skipper, an animal that dines out on rotten cheese and certain kinds of meat, like ham, bacon, and human corpses. The flies are attracted to a by-product of the decomposition process, butyric acid, which has a distinctive acrid/sweet smell (it's also present in vomit). If it seems amazing that a fly can detect a rotting cheese a hundred feet off, consider the fact that the larvae have also been found in cadavers resting in sealed coffins buried nine feet underground. According to Deathonline.com, the animals' carefully judged assessment of a corpse's state of rot makes it a marker for forensic pathologists, who use their presence to determine the approximate time of the host's passing. They're picky, these maggots. *Piophila* expert Dr. Matthew Cobb of the University of Manchester once presented his lab maggots with a ripe Camembert. The creatures wanted nothing to do with it: apparently they didn't care for the smell.

Meanwhile, back at the Sardinian table, the shepherds are covering the roll-ups of casu marzu with their free hand as they go in for a bite. Is it to keep from seeing the larvae? No. Is it to block the smell? No. They're doing it for an entirely different reason: the animals tend to fly in the face of those who would eat them. Exactly how they manage this is best described in charming period terms by William Kirby, in his *Introduction to Entomology* (1815–26):

These maggots have long been celebrated for their saltatorious [jumping] powers. They effect their tremendous leaps—laugh not at the term, for they are truly so when compared to what human forces and agility can accomplish—in nearly the same manner as salmon are stated to do when they wish to pass over a cataract, by taking their tail in their mouth, and letting it go suddenly. When it prepares to leap, our larva first erects itself upon its anus, and then bending itself into a circle by bringing its head to its tail, it pushes forth its unguiform mandibles, and fixes them in 2 cavities in its anal tubercles. All being thus prepared, it next contracts its body into an oblong, so that the 2 halves are parallel to each other. This done, it lets go its hold with so violent a jerk, that the sound produced by its mandibles may be readily heard, and the leap takes place. Swammerdam saw one, whose length did not exceed the fourth part of an inch, jump in this manner out of a box 6 inches deep, which is as if a man 6 feet high should raise himself in the air by jumping 144 feet! He had seen others leap a great deal higher.

The Italian health authorities and the European Union take a very dim view of casu marzu, and routinely crack down on any restaurant owner or market vendor who is brazen enough to sell it in open view. Still, say the guidebooks, it is fairly easy to obtain with the right combination of cash (it goes for three times the going rate of ordinary pecorino) and a studiedly offhand request for the goods they got under the table.

If you are interested in trying casu marzu—for its flavor, its aesthetic appeal, or its reputed aphrodisiac properties—resist the impulse to gulp. If a larva hasn't kamakazeed into your eye, *Piophila casei* has one last trick up its tubercle: if insufficiently chewed up, it can give you a nasty case of intestinal myiasis, in which its mandibles attach and burrow into your intestinal lining, causing dizziness, abdominal pain, and vomiting. Dr. Russell Bonduriansky of the University of New South Wales in Sydney confirms that "the larvae are extremely resistant to toxins in the environment, and are able to survive inside the human digestive tract despite the acids and enzymes produced there." The condition is rare, but several cases are recorded by the Centers for Disease Control and Prevention every year—with more on the way if black-market gastrotours of the Cagliari market start to catch on. The upshot is, if you must eat casu marzu, you don't want it eating you back. Remember to chew at least forty times before swallowing.

Cattail

A certain kind of survivalist out there in the swamp loves cattails because when all hell's breaking loose and the field agents are closing in, the plants provide superior cover. Then there's another kind of survivalist—the kind we're interested in—who loves cattails because they provide superior things for supper. Euell Gibbons was the spiritual leader of the latter camp, a famed wild-food forager and author of the bestselling *Stalking the Wild Asparagus*. He singled out the cattail for praise, saying, "for the number of different kinds of foods it produces there is no plant, wild or domesticated, which tops the common cattail."

It's got lots to offer, and it's got it year-round. The live-off-the-lander can jump into some waders and head to the marshland in spring, summer, autumn, and winter, safe in the knowledge that he'll bring something edible back home. Gibbons elaborates:

When the young plants are about two feet high it is time to gather "Cossack asparagus," so-called because the Russians of the Don are so fond of this food. If one grasps the inside leaves and pulls, the tender inside portion will usually break clean from the root and slip out. Peeled down still further, there is revealed a very tender white part, up to a foot long. This can be eaten either raw or

and go for it. The taste is unexpectedly nice—a limey, garlicky, spicy munch. Hell, you might even reach into your pocket and buy some.

Officially classed as short-horned grasshoppers, chapulines are a standout member of the class of Mexican food known as pre-Hispanic—dishes enjoyed by the Mayans, Aztecs, and, in this locality, Zapotecs, before the Spanish came on the scene. While other pre-Hispanic specialties are found only in specialized restaurants, chapulines are ubiquitous in Oaxaca's markets, restaurants, and bars, particularly during the rainy season from May through October, when they are harvested.

Susana Trilling, director of the Seasons of My Heart cooking school in Oaxaca, in southern Mexico, describes the harvest of chapulines from the fields: "They are found in the corn and alfalfa. They say that chapulines taste of one or another of these grains, depending on where they are harvested. The nets are made from sugar bags (*costales*) . . . sometimes a hoop is placed around the end to make a round wide opening."

The trapped insects are then held for a day so they purge digested matter from their system. Next, according to Susana, they're "boiled, washed, then dry-fried in a skillet with garlic and lime (usually blended), salt and chile, either blended as well or used whole, until the chapulines are really dry. Then they are eaten, as a *botana* (by the handful, as an appetizer), or made into tacos with guacamole and lime and salsa on *blandas* (soft tortillas) or *tlalludas* (larger, more chewy and longer-cooked tortillas), that are unique to Oaxaca."

Chapulines have a spicy, tangy flavor that is an ideal accompaniment to tequila or a cold Victoria beer or the

Oaxacan specialty, *mezcal*. Their texture is pleasant, not so much crunchy as resilient, like firmly cooked wild rice.

But a word of warning is in order. As intriguing as this pre-Hispanic delicacy is to discover, it, like mezcal, is best enjoyed in moderation. In 2003, California physician Dr. Eric Sanford discovered unusually high lead levels in one of his child patients. The origin of the lead was traced to chapulines originating from the state of Oaxaca, a snack that in some cases contained 2,300 micrograms of lead per gram: 383 times the level deemed acceptable for children. It's not clear whether the lead was environmental in origin (due to the proximity of mines) or culinary (the insects may have been cooked in vessels with lead glazing).

So should one avoid chapulines altogether? In our risk-averse world, many would say yes. For his part, Dr. Sanford says this: "I would not give grasshoppers to a child but nor would I worry about an adult eating a handful just once. When one goes to most restaurants on the central square of Oaxaca City they will find chapulines on the menu. They are nice with a cold beer. I wouldn't make a habit of them."

Chicken's Foot

You want to entertain your prospective in-laws when you meet them for the first time at a nice dim sum restaurant in Chinatown. Someone orders chicken's foot. You know that on the back of the foot is a tendon. If you can get at it and pull it just so, you can make the toes clench and release in a comical fashion.

The spring-loaded action comes courtesy of the network of muscles, tendons, ligaments, bone, and thick casing of skin that makes a chicken foot such a gelatinous, gummy, chewy way to pass time at the table. If you like working meat off a bone, it's a good bet you'll love chicken's foot, especially if it's prepared nicely, i.e., deep-fried first, then braised in a tasty sauce. Chicken's foot aficionados are especially passionate about the soft metatarsal pad at center bottom. Gnawers insist that chicken's foot tastes best with the foot bones left in. In the alternative presentation, the pale, vaguely reptilian, scaled flesh is stripped off and dressed in a marinade, offering much less variation in texture. It is a bit like eating moist shed snakeskin, or shreds of rubber chicken hauntingly suffused with chicken flavor.

Chicken's foot is one of those far-flung parts, like pig's snout and oxtail, that was once routinely prepared as part of the family dinner, especially when the family raised animals for the table. Nowadays we favor less anatomically identifiable cuts of meat. Tails, snouts, feet, and trotters are ground beyond recognition and stuffed into sausages or, in the case of chicken's foot, used to make chicken flavoring.

Chicken's foot (and its cousins, duck and goose web) is still routinely prepared in the Chinese kitchen. It also remains a fixture of traditional Jewish cooking, with the feet added to the stockpot to enrich chicken soup. The rendered fat and collagen give the broth a particularly silken consistency, plus there's the entertainment factor of watching the foot do acrobatics through the simmering water.

When you eat chicken's foot, do so in a clean restaurant. This offers some insurance that it has been prepared to a good standard, important with a foodstuff that spent most of its past life ankle-deep in droppings. In a good kitchen they will also clip the toenails, but if they haven't, you might get some use out of one as a toothpick at the end of the meal. This feature of the chicken's foot, by the way, is the inspiration behind its most commonly used alias in Chinese restaurants: "phoenix claws."

If you're inclined to guffaw at such flights of fancy on the menu, goof around with chicken tendons in front of your elders, and pick at your teeth with a chicken's toenail, you might be interested to learn of an experiment recently conducted at the University of South Wales, and reported in the July 2005 issue of *Psychological Science*. "The ability to behave in a socially appropriate way was assessed by asking seventy-one participants to eat a chicken's foot under conditions of high and low social pressure."

That woman you thought was your fiancée's mother? She was actually a research psychologist, hired by your beloved to test your social skills. And guess what! You failed! The marriage is off! Stop playing with your food at the table.

Clay

Down south they do it, especially after a driving rain pelts the earth after a long spell without. "You just have to have it," a woman tells researcher C. J. Forsyth. "If it rains it really makes it, especially if it's real dry. That smell, I can't explain it. I don't know." What she's talking about is dirt, eaten in the raw or cooked and seasoned. In the United States, the habit is particular to rural African American women; a habit they share with women and children all over the world.

We all used to eat dirt with similar gusto. Gerald N. Callahan, associate professor of Immunology/Public Understanding of Science at Colorado State University, writes "eating dirt appears nearly universal among children under two years of age." The Environmental Protection Agency estimates that kids in the United States take in a pinchful—on average about 200 to 800 milligrams a day. This means toddlers are downing the equivalent of a teaspoon of earth every week.

To the vast relief of their parents, most stop taking nips from the sandbox around the age of two. But some adults, primarily women of childbearing age and beyond, can't let it go. They take dirt both as a snack and as a medicine, and oddly enough, it seems to provide real health benefits.

Different localities have different ways of dishing it up. In Haiti, dirt is mixed with margarine, salt, and bouillon powder, formed into small cakes, baked in the sun, and sold as a cheap snack called *argile* or *terre* (French for "earth"). In southern Togo, women of the Ewe tribe have created a cottage industry of harvesting clay from the local hills, washing and processing the slurry, and selling the egg-shaped finished products at the local markets. Elsewhere in Africa, the calcium-rich red soil of termite mounds is carried in a belt and dipped into through the day as a pick-me-up. In the United States, the Culver City–based California Earth Minerals sells clay in powder and pill form as a health supplement.

Officially known as geophagy, soil eating is a subcategory of a broader condition called pica, where nonfood items ranging from hair to feathers to paint chips to laundry starch are eaten to the point of compulsion. While disturbed mental health drives many of these cases, scientists have come around to the idea that an occasional mouthful of dirt may not be so crazy at all.

Researchers agree that the habit is widespread, especially among pregnant women and children, but they can't agree on why this is so. It's the minerals, claim some. People instinctively know to get them from soil, particularly the iron, calcium, zinc, and potassium that otherwise may be lacking in subsistence-level diets. A team of scientists writing in the *Journal of Experimental Biology* offers an alternative theory: after studying kaolin clay's effect in a purpose-built mechanical digestive system, they concluded that this material, which uncoincidentally happens to be the major component of kaopectate, the antidiarrheal medication, sticks to the gastrointestinal lining, hindering the absorption of harmful toxins. It also slows the rate of digestion, reducing the risk of undernourishment and diarrheal dehydration. In other words, clay both settles the system and shields it against bad bugs. A third theory is suggested by Gerald Callahan in a 2003 article for the Centers for Disease Control and Prevention. He suggests that eating dirt might stimulate the immune system of the expectant mother to produce more antibodies against local pathogens (worms, bacteria, etc.) and those antibodies could be passed to the fetus through the placenta. That could help protect the fetus from some of the infections it would likely encounter immediately after birth.

Researchers are quick to add that eating the wrong soil can be a high-risk behavior. Parasitic worms, often present in dog and cat feces, can cause nasty infections of the viscera, eyes, and lungs. Another potentially devastating component of soil can't be seen with a microscope: PCBs and other types of toxic waste that are time bombs once absorbed by the tissues. Nonlethal but nonetheless uncomfortable is the constipation or complete blockage that results from eating too much of even the purest of clays.

The taste of soil is variously reported as sour, salty, or chalky, depending on where it originates and how it's prepared. According to a 1984 survey by D. A. Frate, two-thirds of the earth eaters questioned said they stove-cooked or baked their clay. Salt, vinegar, or other seasonings might be added for extra punch. It's not the kind of food you make an entire meal of. Instead it's a nosh, eaten from a bag or dish, powdery to the fingertips, pleasantly gritty, then mealy in the mouth, habit-forming.

Says one clay lover, speaking to C. J. Forsyth, "It's crunchy, it's satisfying, it's like a craving or something. You get used to it like a candy bar or something like that you really like . . . and there is nothing else that will surpass the taste."

Coconut

✂ 📖

Pity the poor solo round-the-world yachtsman. His sixty-foot monohull caught a rogue wave in the middle of the Pacific, about fifteen degrees south of the equator. The mast snapped clean off and the vessel went down, along with his communications links and GPS device. His last lucid thought before unleashing from his harness was that he should have spent the extra $6,400 on a Breitling emergency watch, which would have broadcast his position to all receivers in a 160-kilometer radius. But he didn't. Sucked into the vortex, he passed a very uncomfortable night bobbing at sea before washing up on the sand of some tiny, nameless island.

After dragging himself into the shade and getting a couple hours' sleep, he drifts back to consciousness, checks his aching bones for breaks, and eventually stands, groggy but intact. The ordeal has left his tongue swollen to twice its normal size, his lips as gritty as sandpaper. It is imperative to find fresh water, for without it, he will live no longer than five days. He slowly walks through the palm trunks that mark the edge of the vegetation of the island's interior. Four hours later, for lack of anyplace better to go, he returns to his patch on the beach, trying to ward off panic. No streams. No springs. Not a cloud in the sky, and no hope of rain anytime soon. He throws himself back against the matted dried fronds, watching the dazzling light scatter through the swaying crowns. It's possible he missed something—a tiny rivulet, a pool of standing rainwater. In a little while, when his strength returns, he'll try again.

Just as his eyes close and his mind starts to drift, a thud concusses two inches to the left of his head, kicking a spray of sand on his face. He wipes away the grains and stares. With its smooth pale husk it doesn't look anything like the hairy brown specimens in the exotic section of the produce aisle, but he's seen its kind before, for sale harborside on Aruba, Maui, Tahiti—a staple of equatorial commerce. A coconut. It could have broken his nose. But it could also save his life. He recalls the deft machete of the vendor in Ocho Rios, who tapped the coconut like a soft-boiled egg, dunked in a straw, and presented the vessel brimming with juice, which had such a comforting, malty-sweet flavor, like weak Ovaltine. His parched throat aches at the memory.

He bounds to his knees, picks the fruit up, and gives it a shake. No slosh—a good sign that it is healthy and filled with liquid. Enough, he vaguely recalls, to keep his kidneys functioning for an entire day. But he doesn't have a knife, much less a machete, how the hell will he open it? He tucks it under an arm and races off to the interior, to the volcanic outcrop that sliced the soles of his high-performance deck shoes so badly earlier in the day. There:

a jagged, sharp-sided wedge, sticking into the air like the tip of a stone iron. He can use it to get started. With the nut in two hands, he brings the base down hard, gouging the outer husk. And again. And again. Chips from the casing fly off, sweat stains his eyes. He flips the nut over and repeats the process, realizing that he must look like a deranged ape, but with each crash of nut against rock he grows more desperate to reach the prize within. After about twenty blows, he senses that the casing is beginning to shear off. He tears at it with his hands, nails packing green with mashed residue. Finally his palms cradle the inner nut, its fibrous casing the final obstacle to the sweet meat within. He turns the nut around in his hands, seeing the three pores at the base that form a small face, the Portuguese *cocos*, or goblin, that gave the nut its name. Knowing these pores to be vulnerable to a sharp tool, he rams the base against the rock to open a crack from which he can drink. But he

misjudges the strike and is left with half of the shell in each shaking hand, the liquid spilled useless into the crags.

Bleak, our man pries a piece of white meat out of the interior and slowly chews, grateful for the tiny bit of moisture that remains behind. But after another piece, and another, he feels his stomach seize with cramp and can no longer swallow the mealy paste. Liquid is critical. He picks his way back to his spot over-looking the sea, the remains of the nut in his hands. He lies back exhausted and stares up, the pink contrail of a jet picked out by the setting sun mocking his isolation. He shifts his glance to the silhouettes of five more nuts in the tree above. The neighboring palm has at least three. They are immature: both good news and bad. Good because the meat inside will be soft and much more easily digested than its riper counterpart, so soft it can be peeled away with a thumbnail. The bad news is that the nut won't be landing anytime soon; he'll have to get up there and fetch it. If he survives the night.

After a terrible sleep filled with dreams about the champagne drenchings that greet winning yachtsmen, he slowly sits up, head throbbing due to dehydration, and considers the tree he is about to try to climb. It is at least seventy feet tall without a single branch between root and crown. Unlike his now-sunken mast, there are no footholds to be seen. He once set anchor in Saipan, Micronesia, during that country's annual games. One of the events was coconut-tree climbing. The contestants, burly men with torsos as tough and brown as old-fashioned catchers' bibs, scrambled up the trunks in seconds.

Though his memory of the event is dim, he recalls that they did it in one of two ways. Some of the men clutched the trunk like a tea-dance escort holds an old lady: hands poised one above the other on what would be the tree's spine, arms nearly straight, body leaning backward. In this way they literally walked up the trunk, always having three points of contact pushing or pulling while the free limb gained altitude upward. The other technique involved wrapping one arm around the back of the trunk while pressing the forearm and palm of the other arm hard against the front. The arches of the bare feet were clamped on opposite sides of the tree, knees bent. In one smooth move, the legs straightened with the feet held tight; once the arms repositioned securely the feet were drawn up and reclamped. In this way the climber hitched straight up.

Our yachtsman takes a good hour and a half longer than the Micronesian gamesmen to get within grabbing range of the coconuts. Streaming with sweat and dizzy from the effort, he is grateful to find that the nuts twist easily off, for his limbs are quaking so hard any defter movement would be impossible. Not taking any chances, he knocks three down to the beach. The descent down the iron-hard bark, which he figured would be easier than the climb, rips inch-wide strips of skin off his chest and upper arms, but he doesn't care, he'll tend to the wounds after he's had something to drink.

This time he takes far more care with the inner shell. Despite the doubling and tripling of his vision, he searches long for just the right tool, a long, glassy-sharp piece of obsidian sturdy enough to withstand the blows of another stone acting as a hammer. Holding the coconut between his knees, the sailor patiently works downward, eventually cracking an opening wide enough for his mouth. He drains the liquid down, shudders, and curls up around his remaining coconuts, exhausted.

After two weeks, he has become so adept at the climbs that when his rescuers finally arrive, attracted by the SOS he spelled out with the discarded husks on the beach, he insists on taking a coconut along. Not to eat, but to plant, in his backyard in Palm Beach.

Cordyceps

A lowly worm or an even lowlier fungus? Such is the mystery of *Cordyceps sinensis*, an inch-long twiglike item that, on closer inspection, looks like a caterpillar wearing a long wizard's cap. The Chinese, who have been on eating terms with it for centuries—following the example of the Tibetans, who have documented it as a medicine since at least the fifteenth century—call it *dongchong xiacao*, or "summer grass/winter worm." The name offers no help in determining cordyceps's true nature as an animal or a vegetable, but at least it takes mineral out of the running.

For clarification, we need to turn to Daniel Winkler, whose paper on *Cordyceps sinensis* in the book *Wildlife and Plants in Traditional and Modern Tibet* reveals all. Cordyceps, nature's ultimate fusion food, comes into the world as a caterpillar, the larva of a ghost moth species native to the

Tibetan plateau. The adult ghost moth has its own peculiarities, namely a lifespan of only a few days, and the utter inability to eat. But the caterpillar can chow down and then some, on the root systems of native grasses. It does this for several years, stopping only to hibernate deep underground when winter comes.

Life is good for the caterpillar unless it's beset by the killer spores of the cordyceps fungus, which, come spring, are thick in the air. Thirty-two million strong may launch from a single fungal fruiting body, sailing the winds and landing upon a victim with the sole agenda of burrowing in and eating the worm hollow. Here Winkler describes the process in detail: "A cotton-like mesh composed of white threads (hyphae) develops inside the body of the insect, first feeding on the less vital parts, until it has taken over the complete organism, filling the caterpillar with its hyphae. After the insect is completely mummified and emptied of nutrients . . . the fungus will develop a fruiting body out of the head above the eyes, where the larva has a horn-like protuberance in the early spring."

In short, the caterpillar becomes a mere shell of its former self, filled with mushroom stuffing. Come cordyceps harvesttime on the Tibetan plateau, the herding and planting is put on the back burner in favor of hunting for fruiting bodies, which poke out of the ground above the shallow graves of the ghost moth larvae. Armed with small shovels, men and women scour the earth for the hard-to-see caps. Driving the effort is the knowledge that once cleaned and dried, the summer grass/winter worm commands a most rewarding price at the wholesale markets in the larger towns. Here the product is packed by the bushel and sent on to China, where traditional Chinese medicine (and, increasingly, double-blind scientific study) holds that cordyceps is a valuable healing agent.

In China, the line between food and medicine is often indistinct. Cordyceps appears on restaurant menus as a stuffing for chicken. It is also made into a tonic soup—one that addresses specific medical complaints at the same time that it satisfies the appetite. There are a range of tonic soups in the Chinese repertoire and they typically contain a potlatch of ingredients such as dried berries, dried herbs, chicken or pork or shellfish, plus a headliner exotic like a handful of dried sea horses, scorpions, or cordyceps. If the latter happens to be the tonic soup of the day, it is probably being ordered for respiratory complaints, general sluggishness, or impotence. Perhaps the worm's extreme rigor in its mortis helps its reputation in this regard. In any case, Tibetan men like to needle the Chinese on the impotence issue, claiming that in Tibet they never have to take the soup for this reason.

In restaurants, tonic soups are often difficult to get on the spot because they must be simmered for at least a couple hours to plump out the dried ingredients and release all the medicinal goodness. Typically, diners call a day ahead to order them.

As an eating experience, it is undramatic. The cordyceps texture is more resilient than you'd expect from a mushroom and less crumbly than you'd expect from a mummy. It tastes like the broth it's been floating in for the past half day.

As food goes, cordyceps is a bit ho-hum, but as a medicine, it has the attention of the orthodox establishment. Remember when Chinese women runners smashed world records in 1993? Accusers cried performance-enhancing drugs. Their coach claimed excellent training and cordyceps tonic. Intriguing results have turned up with laboratory tests of the fungus—showing that it boosts immune cells and it helps kidney patients handle their antibiotics. In one trial it had another effect, at least upon rabbits: they gained weight, markedly so in their testicles. Sperm count also increased. Which raises an interesting question: could it be that the Chinese men who have long been the butt of Tibetan jokes are having the last laugh after all?

Corn Smut

As far as U.S. agribusiness is concerned, corn smut fungus—*Ustilago maydis*—is a blight. It attacks ears of corn and warps them beyond recognition, laying waste to entire fields at a time. The spores reside in the soil, sometimes for years, only becoming active after heavy rain. They seek breaks on the plants caused by wind, hail, or bugs. When the spores reach the kernels, they hijack them, feeding on the juices and distending the pearly niblets to dusky, obscenely misshapen versions of their former selves. To say these ears are disfigured is to wildly understate the situation. Essentially, they are the whole-grain equivalent of the Elephant Man. Eventually, when there are no nutrients left, the spores burst out, leaving the ballooned kernels fluttering spent on the cob.

South of the border in Mexico, farmers see things differently. When they find corn smut in their fields they rejoice. There the symbiotic fungal growth is called *huitlacoche*. It's pared off the cob and used as a rich mushroomy flavoring, as it has been since Aztecs first put it to the pot. Considered a delicacy, it commands a premium price at the market.

For cooking purposes, huitlacoche is best when the spore clumps look shiny silver and feel smooth, dry, and springy to the touch. At this point Mexican cooks gently peel back the surrounding husks, remove the silk, and cut away chunks from the cob with a sharp knife, retaining any kernels—normal-size or grotesque—that adhere to the fungus. Huitlacoche is then briefly sautéed and used as a condiment, adding a earthy, fungal savor to scrambled eggs, soups, quesadillas, and any other dish in which a mushroom would feel at home. Fresh huitlacoche is generally more rich in flavor than the canned, which may have tangy overtones due to the acid preservative.

Unfortunately, in the United States, fresh huitlacoche is difficult to find, though farmers' markets in localities with a sizable Central American population may offer it on a seasonal basis. The canned version is often stocked in the Mexican food sections of big supermarkets. A word of warning to prospective cooks: the picture you see on the label will be exceedingly flattering to the contents within. Huitlacoche disintegrates when it's cooked or processed, turning into an inky, liquid gloop of an unappetizing consistency and suspicious deep brown hue. Its appearance is further blemished by the bloated corn kernels. Frankly, it looks pretty evil. The Aztecs didn't name it "black excrement" for nothing. Another warning: as it heats in a frying pan, it sputters, sending hot inky spore blobs flying around the kitchen.

In an attempt to deflect attention from huitlacoche's dubious appearance and smutty origins, promoters have dubbed it Mexican truffle, Aztec caviar, or maize mushroom. Please. If we must use nicknames, let's stick with black excrement, in honor of the pre-Hispanic farmers who knew good shit when they saw it.

Cricket

✳ ☹ ◉

If you'd like a sundowner, Lao-style, ask your tuk-tuk driver in Vientiane to take you to the Sunset Bar on the banks of the Mekong River. He may look puzzled, for it's not as well known to locals as it is to tourists and ex-pats. You can guide him by urging him onward as you travel north on the river road, until you come to a dirt path. Then it's another kilometer or so down the leafy thoroughfare, past cart vendors set up atop the levee, mom-and-pop restaurants across the road, small guesthouses, a parked '69 Mustang with racing stripes on the hood and sides, a disco playing ballads. When you can go no farther, you've reached the Sunset.

Once you're seated on the back porch, facing the river, soothe your dust-parched throat with a Beerlao tallboy, and let your bones settle back into place after the bumpy ride in the motorcycle's trailing cart. Listen to the waves lap gently against the red mud banks, the faint dialogue from the widescreen in the kitchen, the louder dialogue, in French, English, Lao, and Russian from the nearby tables. Sometimes it gets very loud indeed, especially when an American is defending the national honor against those who believe his country is the new evil empire. But no matter. You're here for the atmosphere, not the politics, and that the place has aplenty—in some ways it's a classic beach bar with its wooden planks, thatched roof where geckos play hide-and-seek, and easygoing attitude. Easygoing is big in Laos. As the saying here goes, *boh pnyang*—no worries.

If you've come this far, you've come for these things, plus one more: a bar snack that makes stale nachos look very lame indeed. You hear that the Sunset Bar serves some of the best fried crickets on the planet. Unlike the batches sold ready-to-eat in the market, they're fresh, and fresh-cooked, not sitting around for days in their own greasy palm oil. About twenty-five come on an oblong dish, deep-fried and garnished with a heap of fried basil. Alongside the crickets comes a small bowl of chili dipping sauce, as well as a basket of sticky rice that you roll into balls with your right hand and eat as the starch component of the meal. But back to the crickets. You pop one into your mouth—legs, head, and all. Hot, just-cooked, it is pure splintering crunch, like the crispiest piece of crispy-duck skin, or a piece of popcorn that has not fully blown out of its hull.

If you're lucky, Pablo will be in the bar. A Filipino architect who's lived in Laos for years, he knows many fine local stories. One of the best is about the *naga*. This is a legendary fish that lives in the Mekong, whose image decorates many of the local Buddhist temples. The animal is shaped like an eel, has big bulgy eyes, and—this is where it gets really good—is some twenty meters long. Sounds like a tall tale? Yes, if it weren't for a couple of Marines based in Laos during the Secret War. They actually managed to catch one. There are photographs. The sucker really is that big. What's more, says Pablo, drawing deep on his cigarette, it breathes fire. On one evening a year, in October (the monks know the exact date, which changes from year to year), about sixty kilometers upriver, it's possible to see the spectacle. It takes place deep in the countryside, but people gather along the banks to see where exactly the bursts will originate—it could be anywhere, it's a very wide river. Once, twice, twenty times, an orange tracer will shoot from the water to a few feet above it. Pablo has seen it himself. He's a rational man. The monks, who have a great deal of clout in local matters, will not allow scientific study of any kind.

Before you know it, you've nearly polished off the crickets. How did *that* happen? You're of two minds about this. It's kind of cool that you just ate a plate of bugs, but it's not something you really care to dwell on. It probably didn't hurt that you arrived just at sunset, and your dish was hard to discern in the lowering dusk. As you finish the last one, think of the naga. Its story is as strange as your liking for crickets—some mysteries just are, and best stay, unsounded.

Dog

"Anyone who would eat pig and not eat dog is a total hypocrite." So says an American consultant living in Seoul, Korea, underlining dog's status as the most polarizing food on the planet. Even cultures that ate the animal ritualistically show evidence of being divided on the issue. In his *Food: A History*, Felipe Fernández-Armesto cites an article by W. K. and M. M. N. Powers on an archaic Oglala Sioux custom:

The dog-feast is an enactment of divine order, the slaughter preceded by a lament for the loss of a friend. Anointed with a line of red paint to symbolize "the red road, which . . . represents all that is beneficial in the world," the dog is made to face west, to be garrotted by women who stand on either side of it, pulling a rope around its neck, while the medicine man administers a blow from behind. "The act of killing the dog is likened to being struck by lightning and guarantees that the spirit of the dog will be released in order to go to the west where it will join the thunder people, those spirits who have powers over life and death, and themselves are symbolized by lightning." The meat is boiled without seasonings: this is a cross-cultural feature of sacred food, which is eaten not for savour but for salvation.

In recent times, the battle line between canine consumers and the opposition has been most sharply drawn in Korea, where dog is served in an estimated six thousand restaurants to an estimated three million diners, making it the country's fourth most popular meat (after beef, pork, and chicken). There the most famous dog dish is *poshintang*, a popular midsummer restorative—literally "body preservation stew." Advocates claim it helps speed a sluggish or ailing metabolism (dog restaurants are often found near hospitals). Convalescents drink it to regain their health, as do men hoping to retrieve their lost bone, metaphorically speaking.

The Korean government, eager to buff the country's image shortly before the Seoul Olympics in 1988, banned the sale of dog meat as "unsightly." But after the closing ceremonies wrapped up and spectators left the city, restaurants serving dog reemerged. Back again, the proprietors were nonetheless aware of their status as an endangered species. When the World Cup soccer tournament was slated to take place in Seoul in 2002, they decided to take the offensive. The eyes of the world would be on Korea and its dining habits. The dog meat sellers decided to launch a classic PR campaign on their own behalf. One hundred restaurant owners would hold a convention at which foreign guests would be introduced to the meat's delights. Dr. Ahn Yong-kuen of Chungchong University was enlisted as a spokesman, thanks to his lengthy list of credentials, including one book and four academic papers extolling dog as a food, and 350 recipes in his card file. Promptly dubbed "Dr. Dog Meat" by the press, he was positioned against seasoned animal-rights campaigner and former sex kitten Brigitte Bardot, who has made no friends in Korea with statements like "a cultured country does not allow its people to eat dogs."

The ultimate showdown never took place. Under mysterious circumstances, the government-owned management company of the convention hall canceled the event just before its scheduled opening. Dr. Dog Meat hasn't been heard from since, at least on the international stage. For their part, the restaurateurs have refused to roll over, holding dog meat festivals in Seocheon and other villages around the country, bringing in their vanloads of posters, cookbooks, dog oil, and meat. Protesters, too, are an inevitable feature of these events.

While some of the objectors are "dogs are people too" types, who believe that eating this animal is tantamount to cannibalism, others are less troubled by the actual consumption than they are by the animals' treatment prior to and during the killing. In an industry as unregulated as the dog meat trade, cruel and unhygienic conditions are inevitable. Worse, since some diners believe that the flavor of dog meat is enhanced by adrenaline just prior to slaughter, the animals may be beaten or otherwise tormented before they are killed. Animal rights websites abound with photographs of overpacked cages and hacked-apart animals bleeding on concrete.

The sourcing of the animals is also—to put it mildly—disreputable. In his book *Strange Foods*, author Jerry Hopkins cites a 1997 *Nation* article that says, "in most countries where dog is eaten, farming is not necessary, as strays and other unwanted canines are plentiful. For this reason there are men like [Thai dogcatcher] Chavalit Phorak, who travels the back roads and barters for dogs, then sells the meat, entrails and skins. 'My truck has a loudspeaker,' he said. 'Everywhere I go I tell people that I will give them pails for their naughty or lazy dogs.'"

Phorak's implication is that dogs are voluntarily given away. But dognapping is also a possibility if the owner is not at the other end of a leash. In dog-eating areas of the world, which include China, Taiwan, Myanmar, Indonesia, Laos, Vietnam, Ghana, and the Congo, traffic isn't the only reason you don't let a family pet roam the streets.

Which makes the spectacle of food tourists seeking out dog meat shops along Nhat Tan dike in Vietnam, or in Baguio City in the Philippines, or the hot-pot restaurants of Shanghai, such a tooth-and-nail topic. They're not starving, like the Norwegian explorer Roald Amundsen and his men, who ate up their husky team on the race to the South Pole. They're not ailing, like the many Koreans who eat poshintang with the hope of achieving a health turnaround. They're not even in for a phenomenal meal, as dog is typically described as a porky-tasting meat prone to being stringy, tough, and/or greasy, depending on the animal's age and the cooking method.

So are these people fearless gourmets or callous gluttons or something else altogether? Wherever you come down on this particular argument, it is one worth having, because outside of vegetarian quarters, the heart so rarely enters the domain of the stomach.

Dragonfly

In Bali, they like their dragonflies dewinged, beheaded, and fried in coconut oil until crisp. It's a quick snack, but the Balinese stalkers are quicker still. They snag the animals at the end of a long stick that's been dipped in the sticky latex of the jackfruit tree.

Lightning-fast reflexes and patience are the hallmarks of dragonfly catchers, for these animals—the ultimate hunters of fellow insects—are brilliantly equipped to elude capture themselves. Their advantages start with massive eyes, each thirty thousand lenses strong and capable of spotting a mosquito forty feet off. Each of their four wings is, uniquely in the insect kingdom, able to beat out of phase, meaning independently of one another. Wind-tunnel-and-smoke experiments upon tethered dragonflies demonstrate that the animals generate unsteady airflow over their wings, microturbulence that reduces air pressure and amplifies lift. This translates into the ability to fly at thirty-five miles per hour, stop dead and hover, fly backward, and do loops. Internally, the insect's cardiac system is suspended in a liquid-filled sac, which works like a top gun's flight suit. The dragonfly is the only animal that can withstand 30 g of lateral force (trained fighter pilots start blacking out at 4). Their aerodynamics give them an unparalleled prey-intercept rate (measured by researchers as high as 97 percent), a barnstorming sex life, and the ability to lead pursuers on quite the splashy chase through the wetlands.

If you are interested in capturing a dragonfly without harming the creature—and you don't want to hurt it, lest all the mosquitoes it was destined to eat come find your sorry hide instead—there are alternatives to the sticky-stick snare. One is to form a tennis-racquet-sized loop from a supple branch like a willow, twisting the ends together to make a handle, and dip the face of the loop through several disused spiders' webs, covering the frame with filaments. The next step is to sneak up on your quarry and gently swish it into the sticky trap. Successful sneaking up, never mind capture, will take practice.

Even more so the hand-capture method, devised by dragonfly expert Soowon Cho and described on the International Odonata Research Institute's website:

Approach the dragonfly very slowly from the front, watching the dragonfly's head and legs for signs of disturbance. If the dragonfly tenses, freeze until it appears to relax. When you get within about 5 feet of the dragonfly, slowly extend your arm out to the side and slowly rotate the arm in the vertical plane like a clock hand while continuing to slowly approach the dragonfly. As you get progressively closer, reduce the radius of the circle your arm is making (by angling your arm forward from your body) so that your hand, pointer finger extended, slowly spirals in toward the dragonfly. The dragonfly should track the motion of your hand by rotating its head. If your movements are slow and steady, it may be mesmerized and not take alarm and fly away. When your fingers are within a couple inches of the dragonfly, quickly grasp it by the wings (or whatever else you can get ahold of between thumb and forefinger or between fore and middle finger).

Alternatively, wait until dark. Use a flashlight to check the undersides of leaves near the dragonflies' favorite watering hole. Grasp any you may find firmly and gently, in an unhurried fashion, while they're still fast asleep.

The last method is efficient, but it's hardly sporting. To experience the true pleasures of a dragonfly hunt, do it while your prey is awake, and wondering why all thirty thousand of you are slowly rotating your arms in the vertical plane . . .

Dung Beetle Larvae

A dung beetle walks into a bar. "Pardon me," he says to the bartender. "Is this stool taken?"

In many areas of the world, people eat bugs on a routine basis. Thailand is one such place. But even in Thailand, where deep-fried bamboo worms are scarfed down like Cheez Doodles, people just say no to certain kinds of insect. In the northern and northeastern part of the country, for example, the Thai are kind of freaked by the Lao ethnic group's penchant for eating dung beetles and their larvae.

For their part, the Lao overlook the bugs' dodgy accommodations and matter-of-factly pick them out for the table. Good enough to eat, they are here. Other cultures hold them in an even higher regard, elevating them to a central place in their worldview. Members of the *Onitis, Oryctes,* and *Copris* genuses—all eaten in Asia—are classed within the greater Scarabaeidae family. In ancient Egypt, scarab beetles rolling balls of dung across the sands inspired the myth of the sun god Ra. Some modern Egyptologists believe that the beetles also inspired the practice of wrapping up dead nobles and sealing them in pyramids, for during their time of metamorphosis, the larvae seal themselves in spheres of dung, from which they emerge reborn. Beautiful ceramic models of the beetles accompanied many a mummy on its journey to the afterlife, and today they are worn in the region as good-luck charms.

Apart from their spiritual associations, dung beetles also perform a vital ecological function, for without their tremendous appetite for waste, the earth would be blanketed in poo. A website called Gordon's Dung Beetle Page describes the action at 1.5 kilograms' worth of elephant dung being staked out by interested observers on the African savanna. "In two hours that small pile of dung attracted 16,000 dung beetles of various shapes and sizes, who between them had eaten and or buried that dung completely."

If you spread it, they will come . . . but somebody still has to dig the dung beetles out. As is usually the case with insect foraging, women and children do most of the work. In a 1975 report entitled *Edible Insects of Northeast Thailand*, cited in Gene DeFoliart's online book *The Human Use of Insects as a Food Resource*, V. Vara-asavapeti and his colleagues explain that the animals

are collected from animal dung piles in the morning, using a shovel and bucket of water. In some villages, signs are placed on certain dung piles to indicate that they are already "reserved." After collection the beetles are left overnight in a bucket of water to rid themselves of the ingested dung. They are also soaked in water for two or three hours before cooking. The beetles sold in markets are cooked with a little salt. Some people eat the beetles whole while others remove the wings first.

Dung beetles and their larvae also figure as a traditional food in Myanmar. Dr. Sein Tu describes the larvae (called *nauchae boe* in Burmese) as "white in color, very rich in protein, and . . . very succulent and tasty when roasted." Again in *The Human Use of Insects as a Food Resource*, Professor DeFoliart recounts a personal conversation with a native of Myanmar. "The larva of the dung beetle, which is enclosed in a globe of earth, is particularly prized. The globe is found some one to three or more feet underground, either singly or in groups of three or more, and entails a lot of hard work to be unearthed. The gooey contents of the larva are squeezed out of the cuticle and cooked with scrambled eggs."

Say you're traveling in remote regions of Southeast Asia. Your host insists on your trying a grub that, you suspect, was once shoveling the shit like there was no tomorrow. You're worried about nasty germs. Here's some advice. Make sure the bug is well cooked. And don't forget to wash your hands first.

Durian

You're having neighbor problems. The girl in the apartment one flight up comes home from her shift at 2:00 a.m. and puts a Dido CD very loudly on endless repeat until sunrise.

One solution is to have a friendly nonconfrontational chat. Another, more pointed, is to counterstrike with Marilyn Manson. But the most scorched-earth of all is to find a ripe durian fruit in the nearest Chinatown, hide it in a wastebasket, leave for a week, and let nature go to work for you. You'll need thick rubber gloves for disposing of the fruit and a gas mask to reinhabit your apartment, but there are compensations. The worst of the smell rises. If she hasn't called the cops on suspicion of a rotting cadaver in the building she'll at minimum think twice about renewing her lease.

In the Far East they call durian the King of Fruits. It grows to the size of a human head and can weigh upwards of ten pounds. Covering the rind are two-inch-long, greenish-brown thorns that will pierce your skin if you underestimate them. When a ripe durian in the forty-meter-high canopy breaks off its bough, it drops like a cannonball. Any obstacle between it and the ground is in for a wallop. Death is a possibility, despite the hard hats the harvesters wear. Since a collision would also mess up the produce, most plantations utilize netting to keep rinds and skulls intact.

Philippine mythology tells how the durian came to be: Once upon a time there was an old and ugly king whose young bride refused to love him. The king, in desperation, turned to a hermit for help. The hermit told the king to fetch three things: the egg of a black tabon bird, twelve ladles of fresh milk, and nectar from the flower of the tree of make-believe. Plant these things in the royal garden, said the hermit, and throw a big feast, inviting me to the celebration. The morning after the items were planted, a tree grew, bearing a beautiful sweet fruit, which the king gave to his bride. She promptly fell in love with him. The king threw his feast but forgot to invite the hermit. The hermit cursed the fruit, turning it spiky and stinky, and forever after it was known as the durian.

The King of Fruits, the Sid Vicious of Fruits—no matter what you call it, durian is wildly popular. It has its own festival in Davao City, Philippines. In Singapore, the Four Seasons Durian Dessert Shop sells countless brands of ice creams, cakes, cookies, candies, puddings, and pastes flavored with durian essence. Durian-flavored candy is found all over Asia, right next to the Mentos and Juicy Fruit. As for the fresh fruit, you always know when you're approaching a durian stall thanks to the sewer stench thick in the air.

What's the big deal about durian? To find out, you have to get past the forbidding exterior. The best way is to hold the fruit in heavy gloves or in a towel, position it so that the point opposite the stem end is facing you, and slice through it, following one of the thorn growth lines. The fruit will fall open with a sickening clunk. Inside, in distinct lobes surrounding large seeds, is the creamy-green pulp, a custardy, slimy mass that's easily scooped with the fingertips (traditional) or a spoon (recommended).

A warning: the taste, for some, is just as revolting as the smell. Once tried, it's never forgotten, a musky, caramelized sweet garlic with faint overtones of strawberry. Durian fans love its deep-brain allure. Aromatically speaking, it's a bit like eating and having sex and going to the bathroom all at the very same time, if that's the kind of thing that you're into.

The smell can cling to fingertips and lips. Durian fans advise swilling a bit of salt water in the empty shell, scraping fingers against the interior, and using this liquid to rinse out the mouth. Chemicals in the rind, they say, act to neutralize the funk. And once you're done with your durian fruit, be sure to take the garbage straight out.

Fat-tailed Sheep Tail

In Uzbekistan and elsewhere in central Asia, the sheep are renowned for the magnificent amplitude of their tails. Baa-baa's got back and then some. It's a survival adaptation of ancient desert breeds like the Karakul and Awassi, similar to a camel's storing fat in its hump. A mature sheep that is grazing well typically boasts a ten-pounder. On some breeds it sticks straight out, like a fifth leg. On others, it's shaped like an S and bumps along behind, like a mini U-Haul trailer.

Herodotus tells of shepherds in times past who "have enough skill in carpentry to make little carts for their sheep's tail. The carts are placed under the tails, each sheep having one to himself, and the tails are then tied down upon them." Traveling on the Silk Road, Marco Polo noted: "there are sheep here as big as asses; and their tails are so large and fat, that one tail shall weigh some thirty pounds." But even these big woollies were underendowed compared to those described by Leo Africanus, writing around 1520: "In Egypt, many persons make a business of fattening sheep, and feed them on bran and wheat, and then the tail gets so big that the sheep can't stir. But those who keep them tie the tail on a kind of little cart, and in this way they move about. I saw one sheep's tail of this kind at Asiot, a city of Egypt . . . which weighed 80 lbs., and many people asserted that they have seen such tails that weighed 150 lbs."

Whether curvy or morbidly obese, the tails provided a reliable source of food fat. If the shepherd was halfway decent with a sharp knife and needle, this commodity was a renewable resource. Writing in AD 250, Aelian describes an Indian technique: "They cut open the tails and take out the tallow, and then sew it up again." For Mongolians and other hordes on the go, outright amputation was a quicker means to an end. The sheep, a hardy animal, was likely to survive the loss, at least until Genghis got a taste for some chops.

Yaweh, for His part, likes tail fat too. In Leviticus 3, Moses makes it quite clear: "You shall present its fat from the sacrifice of well-being, as an offering by fire to the Lord: the whole broad tail, which shall be removed close to the backbone. . . . Then the priest shall turn these into smoke on the altar as a food offering by fire for a pleasing odor. All fat is the Lord's."

If God sounds reluctant to share, it's because this was much more than a survival food. Tail fat was (and is) cherished for its rich muttony taste, its ease of meltability over a wind-blown fire, and the absence of the rank, mouth-coating quality that characterizes the fat from other parts of the animal. Until quite recently, tail fat was as much a staple of central Asian cookery as olive oil is in the Mediterranean. One of the most popular Arabic cookbooks of the middle ages, *Kit'b al-Wusla al-Habib*, lists tail fat as an ingredient in thirty-four recipes. Today, in Uzbekistan and neighboring countries in central Asia, pilafs are a feast food, and a time-honored flavoring is melted fat, possibly mixed with other ingredients like honey or vinegar. Especially in Uzbekistan, notes food historian Russell Zanca, tradition holds that the pilaf is well prepared if the fat runs golden down the arm as it is scooped by hand into the mouth. "He is happiest who is most greasy," wrote one observer centuries ago, and the observation could as easily be made today.

Today, the visitor to an Anatolian town like Konya in Turkey will see tail fat—*dumba*—on a shish kebab, the chunks interspersed between pieces of garlic-marinated lamb meat and slices of onion. The fat roasts golden crisp in the fire, and it is delicious. In Tehran, a visitor to a doner kebab stall might see layers of tail fat interleaved with the meat on the rotating vertical spit, sliced to order and served in a pita. In a *chaikhana*, or Afghanistan teahouse, the specialty might be a bowl of rice strewn with bits of roast meat, with a chunk of broiled fat hiding under the grains, glistening like a jewel, the best saved for last.

Fermented Mare's Milk

According to the Mongolian tourist board, the population density of this central Asian country is about 1.5 people per square mile. If you like your personal space, this is the place to be, but this is not to say that the Mongolian people aren't sociable. In fact, the tradition of friendliness and hospitality to strangers is so deeply entrenched it's not even necessary to knock on the door of a *ger*, the traditional Mongolian felt tent, before entering. Nor do you say "May I come in?" Instead, you shout *Nokhoi khori!* (hold the dog!) and step right in, being careful not to knock down a tent pole.

If it's summertime, look alongside the door for a large hanging leather bag. This is the *hohuur*, and inside it is fermenting mare's milk, called *airag* in Mongolia (and *koumiss* elsewhere in central Asia). It is the height of good manners to give the bag a twirl or a shake as you come and go, for they say airag needs to be agitated a thousand times over its twenty-four-hour fermentation process before it is ready for drinking.

"Drink" is not quite the right word for what rural Mongolians do with airag during its summer season: "glug" comes closer, for it is consumed in huge quantities. It is considered a food as much as a beverage, and it has a mild alcoholic quality (which only takes effect upon being consumed in huge quantities). Make no mistake, this is a party beverage, no matter what the time of day; and it has been ever thus, since herdsmen on these steppes first domesticated the horse.

William of Rubruck, a Flemish monk, set out to Mongolia in the 1250s with the humble aim of converting the residents of the great eastern parts to Christianity. Somebody on high must have been watching over him because he made it intact to the Tartar plains. There he encountered hospitality he saw fit to describe in a letter to King Louis IX:

In summer they care only for cosmos (airag). There is always cosmos near the house, by the entry door. . . . And when the master has drunken . . . then they all drink all around, and sometimes they do drink right shamefully and gluttonly. And when they want to challenge anyone to drink, they take hold of him by the ears, and pull so as to distend his throat, and they clap and dance before him. Likewise, when they want to make a great feasting and jollity with someone, one takes a full cup, and two others are on his right and left, and thus these three come singing and dancing towards him who is to take the cup, and they sing and dance before him; and when he holds out his hand to take the cup, they quickly draw it back, and then again they come back as before, and so they elude him three or four times by drawing away the cup, till he hath become well excited and in good appetite, and then they give him the cup, and while he drinks they sing and clap their hands and strike with their feet. (trans. by W. W. Rockhill, 1900: The journey of William of Rubruck to the eastern parts of the world, 1253–55, as narrated by himself, with two accounts of the earlier journey of John of Pian de Carpine*)*

Partying of this kind is not guaranteed to the contemporary visitor, but you can rest assured that the bowl will be passed time and time again from host to guest within the ger, whose side flaps are lifted during the summer months to bring in light and breeze. You'll hear the occasional whinnies of the mares, which are milked every couple hours to yield about two liters of drink, to which some leftover airag is added as a starter for the fermentation. If left to brew for a day or so, the milk becomes airag, which is slightly effervescent and sour, hitting the tongue tartly but, when properly made, leaves a taste of almonds. A stronger version (up to 18 percent alcohol) results if the beverage is left to mature longer in its sack, or it may be distilled to produce the powerful *arkhi*, or milk brandy.

The guest would do well to remember his manners—you accept the passed cup with both hands, take a sip, and return it to your host. Do not lift your pinkie British tea-parlor style, do not expose your wrists, and do not whistle in the ger, it's considered bad luck. If you can sing, though, you're in great company—the Mongolians are champions of *Urtyn Duu*, or long songs. Settle back and enjoy the twenty thousand verses that may follow—you won't lack for liquid refreshment.

Fighting Bull

↗

The corrida—the death dance—is over, and a thousand pounds' worth of fighting bull is crumpled in the dark wet dirt of the ring. Its aorta has been sliced by the matador's *estoque*, which is plunged to the hilt between its shoulder blades, or, if this didn't work out entirely to plan, its spinal cord severed by a thrust with a second sword behind the head.

The bull was bred for speed, agility, and, above all, aggression. It played its role in the twenty-minute, three-stage drama—provocation by mounted picadors, harassment with the bandilleras' lances, and the goading and final death strike by the matador at close quarters—with fearsome tenacity. But as is almost invariably the case, the matador triumphed (a recent tally of the past forty-five years in Spain shows the matadors winning by 134,000 to

4). The bulls are slaughtered in the name of tradition, of art, and of pragmatism. Once a fighting bull has competed, it becomes wise to the game. If the animal weren't killed with prejudice, it would be overwhelmingly good in its second outing. The animal must be killed at the end of the con-

test, otherwise the odds would tip too far in its favor.

At the end of the show, the dead animal is taken away by a team of horses (if it performed bravely, it is dragged on a triumphal lap around the ring). Before bovine spongiform encephalitis (BSE) hit European cattle, fighting bulls were butchered in the shadow of the arena, and the meat was available for purchase on the spot. Today, health regulations dictate that the animals must undergo brain-tissue tests before the parts are sold, making the purchase of fighting-bull meat a less spontaneous affair. It is still available at select butchers for about four dollars a pound, particularly in bullfighting centers such as Pamplona and Ronda, but it is a specialty product whose presence in the butcher's case is never guaranteed. You may also find fighting bull on the menu in restaurants frequented by aficionados. Odds are, the waiter will be able to tell you the name of the animal that supplied your *raba de toro*, or oxtail stew, as well as the name of the matador that slew him.

The meat from a fighting bull is dark in color, "black"

in the local parlance. This is due to the particular conditions under which it lived and died. Prior to the fight, the animal was transported for many miles, held in an unfamiliar pen close to unfamiliar animals, deprived of food and drink, punctured with a rosette displaying its home ranch's colors, and exposed to the smells of blood and fear of its fellow bulls. With the exception of the rosette, all of these conditions may also be experienced by feedlot cattle destined for the American table. They are factors that our meat industry recognizes as directly responsible for the occurrence of "dark-cutting" beef.

Essentially, dark beef is stressed beef. The color indicates that the muscles' glycogen (energy) reserves have run very low. Low glycogen levels before death translate into lower lactic acid content after. According to Chris R. Calkins, the Nebraska Beef Industry Professor of Animal Science at the University of Nebraska, this causes several things to happen:

The proteins in the meat expand to retain more water, leaving the surface of the meat to feel dry or sticky. Light scattering is low on such a surface, causing a dark appearance. Additionally, oxygen diffusion from the air into the cut surface of the meat is diminished, allowing the non-oxygenated color pigment (called myoglobin) to predominate, further exaggerating the dark color.

U.S. table beef that is dark, rather than the cherry-red consumers prefer, is liable to be demerited up to one full grade in the USDA's rating system, but the problem isn't only cosmetic. This meat is also prone to deteriorate faster, and some tests indicate that it's harder to chew. South Dakota State and Ohio State researchers showed that a sirloin from a dark-cut carcass had a shear force value 33 percent greater than meat of a normal color, meaning that it was a third harder to tear apart.

In the U.S. National Beef Quality audit of 2000, the incidence of dark-cutting meat in all the carcasses surveyed was 2.3 percent. Nobody is surveying fighting-bull carcasses, but it's a good bet that the percentage is close to a hundred. These animals live truly fine lives for the three or four years prior to the corrida—running free in lush pastures and experiencing the world as their gene code intended. But their last days are trying: the transport, the penning, and, obviously, the fight itself.

In Seville, where bullfighting was born in the thirteenth century, the meat of fighting bulls has traditionally been considered inferior. According to Dominique Fournier's article "Bull's Meat," for the online journal Slowfood.com, "Seville has deified the bull, but it still thinks its meat should be reserved for the poor and the down-and-out. The city seems somehow to bear the marks of the period when meat from the bullfight was used as *caridades*, charity in the form of food granted to hospices and prisons by the powerful who wished to keep in God's good books." Or maybe the Sevillanos simply prefer a more tender cut. Apart from any acid-level effects, the meat of fighting bulls is by nature tougher than the typical supermarket-bound steer, not because it's a more hard-ass animal but because it's an older one. Says

Professor Calkins, "Animals that reach puberty, especially bulls, show a significant reduction in tenderness. This is especially true in the connective tissues that are found around and within the muscle." Even the most devoted fighting-bull-meat fan usually enjoys it in the form of a stew, after it's spent many hours tenderizing in a slow pot.

One part—actually a pair of parts—of the fighting bull doesn't profit from long cooking. This is because testicles are glands rather than muscle, and are relatively unaffected by glycogen issues. Called *criadillas*, they are seen as the wellspring of the animal's fighting spirit, and as such have their own potent allure. Recipes recommend an initial parboiling before they are quick-fried or fricasseed, to tenderize and spirit away overly rank odors. Criadillas, unsurprisingly, were the preferred food of the great lover Giacomo Casanova, who called them "his favorite delicacy."

In bullfighting there is a lesser-known tradition that even its most committed opponents might find tolerable. It is called the *indulto*, which means "pardon," and it is granted in the midst of a contest to an animal that has shown exceptional valor against the toreros, or bullfighting team. The bull is symbolically killed, by the empty hand of its opponent, and is then allowed to leave the ring and the city intact. It will go on to become a *semental*, or stud bull, its criadillas destined for alternative duty that Casanova himself could only applaud.

Fly Agaric

Your friendly neighborhood garden gnome—that bearded plastic fellow who lives in frost-hardy plantings the world over—often leans on an accessory: a jaunty red mushroom with white spots on its cap. Little do the good people mulching somewhere nearby know that this particular mushroom has one of the most debauched reputations in the fungal kingdom. The fly agaric, or *Amanita muscaria*, is a legendary intoxicant. It gives flies such a buzz that they slam into walls. It helped Viking despoilers power up into full rape-and-pillage mode. It convinced isolated Siberians to drink one another's urine. But more on its festive side a bit later.

Fly agaric is currently eaten as a food in places like Japan, where it's dried, ground, and sprinkled in soups to add extra savor, or pickled and served as a side dish. When properly prepared, its main psychoactive ingredients, ibotenic acid and muscimol, are cooked off, leaving behind the meaty goodness favored by the discriminating mushroom gourmet. Despite this, almost every mushroom guide you'll come across warns against harvesting it, due to the psychoactive effects it has in its raw state and, more important, its guilt by association with close kin *Amanita phalloides*, better known—especially in emergency-room circles—as the death cap.

It's worth a brief aside to spell out exactly how deadly death cap is. It has been cited as the perpetrator in up to 90 percent of mushroom-related deaths worldwide. It's an extremely efficient killer and, what's worse, it often taunts its victims with false hope. According to Roger Phillips's *Mushrooms and Other Fungi of Great Britain and Europe*, in the first twenty-four hours, symptoms of poisoning include "vomiting, diarrhea, sweating and insatiable thirst, followed by a pale, haggard appearance with cold hands and feet, accompanied by a state of deep anxiety." After this terrible first day, the symptoms let up. The no-longer-anxious victim drops dead a few days later, when the toxins that have been silently grinding the liver and kidneys finally turns them to pulp. If by accident or foul play you have consumed death cap, getting to a doctor quickly is no guarantee of survival; case histories routinely record heroic efforts made on patients' behalf, but these toxins are ruthless.

By comparison, fly agaric's effects are relatively lightweight. If you consume too much of the raw fungus you will experience gastric distress, unpleasant hallucinations, and uncontrollable twitchiness alternating with comatose-deep slumbers. If, despite these symptoms, you stubbornly keep eating it—due to impaired judgment or because you want an even stronger "experience"—there is a chance that it will kill you. It is thought that the American species may be more toxic than the European.

The death cap typically has a greenish or yellow cap, whereas the fly agaric's is red, but this distinction may not be obvious (or even evident) to the amateur 'shroomer stumbling through the pine forest, intent on finding his inner shaman. Fired by tales from the internet and the writings of Harvard ethnobotanist R. Gordon Wasson, these people, like their vision-seeking counterparts of old, are after an all-natural high that, at least in theory, will bring them closer to the world of the spirits.

In his *Soma: Divine Mushroom of Immortality*, Wasson claimed that fly agaric was the mystic soma of the ancient Aryan tribes, a people that 3,500 years ago swept down from the mountains of central Asia into present-day Iran. According to the Rig Veda, their epic collection of hymns, soma was an essential element of religious rites, drunk to bring on a sublime state: "dazzling, flaming, brilliant, resplendent, lustrous." The Rig Veda also recounts that the drink gave the priests very full bladders, which they relieved as part of the rituals.

Which brings us full circle to the Kayak, Chichi, Kanchanalak, Osyka, Vogel, and other peoples of northeast Siberia, who likewise ate *A. muscaria* and relieved themselves, but did the Aryans one better by actually drinking said urine. They did this in the belief that the body absorbed the mushroom's more unpleasant components—for example, the chemical factor that causes twitchiness—while the buzz's premium features passed intact in the flow. The Siberians didn't stop at one filtration: the active elements, they believed, stayed active through up to four passes through the kidneys, and so urine would be pissed and drunk, pissed and drunk all night long, either in a solo effort or shared among friends and hangers-on. In 1736, a Swede named Strahlberg, stuck in Siberia as a prisoner of war for twelve years, wrote: "The poorer sort, who cannot afford to lay down a store of these mushrooms, post themselves, on these occasions, around the huts of the rich, and watch for the opportunity of a guest coming down to make water, and then hold a wooden bowl to receive the urine, which they drink off greedily, as having still some virtue of the mushroom in it, and by this way they also get drunk."

And thus we see how, deep in the frigid Siberian night, three hundred years ago, some stoner first slurred the immortal words, "Hey, man, pass the bowl."

Foie Gras

If you bypass the creamy, cool mouthfeel and really go deep into the flavor, you might find that foie gras takes you back to your grade-school lunchroom. It's a little hazy, but there's this orange and red bag . . . a comical bandit with a Pancho Villa mustache . . . somebody giggling milk out their nose . . . Fritos. Foie gras tastes *a lot* like Fritos. An outlandish suggestion to an old-school gourmand, but it's not entirely unfounded. After you strip away the cultural associations, corn is the principal constituent of both.

Another similarity: corn chips and foie gras are both highly processed. Snack factories are sprawling affairs equipped with mixing vats, conveyor belts, and ovens. Foie gras manufacture begins and ends in complex chemical processes in the liver of the moulard duck (or domestic goose). The physical plants may differ, but both systems have been refined by food technologists to maximize the output of product.

Foie gras means "fat liver" in French, and that's literally what this food is: an organ whose fat cells have multiplied and enlarged well beyond normal limits due to the forced feeding of the surrounding animal.

Some food historians say foie gras' origins trace to ancient spring days on the banks of the Nile. It was here that wild fowl ate voraciously in preparation for their long migration back to Europe. (Modern foie gras birds are able to withstand force-feeding due to their ancestors' genetic predisposition to gorge.) The Roman writer Pliny credits his countryman Metellus Scipio, a governor of Syria in 49–48 BC, for inventing the force-feeding process, which will be detailed momentarily. Sixteen centuries later, again according to gastronomic legend, wandering Jews brought the technique to southern France, where it became known as *gavage*. Enterprising chefs went on to make foie gras a dish much appreciated by Louis XVI, whose own goose was cooked by the French Revolution.

Engorging a foie gras liver to table weight is a carefully orchestrated process. The moulard duck is bred for its relatively low-key and robust nature; it will not sputter about the pen like Donald or Daffy, expending valuable calories on its own outrage. In the first weeks of its life, the duckling is free-range, encouraged to move around and eat grass, which both toughens the esophagus and, due to the amount of clippings necessary to glean reasonable nutrition, stretches it. Then, in stage two of the rearing process, the animal is offered grain mash for four weeks, initially an all-you-can-eat deal that further limbers the esophagus and brings the duck's liver to half the target weight. At this point the duck begins its largely round-the-clock confinement in very tight group quarters or in an individual cage that affords just enough room to eat, drink, and plump to the ground. Meals are quick and calorie-packed, less an all-day picnic than a takeout shoveled in while the car is idling in the parking lot.

The fact is, if humans could eat meals the way a foie gras bird can, whole new worlds of time would open up for us. In the final two weeks of rearing, the animals get two or three daily visits from the farmhand, who approaches with a thirty-centimeter-long flexible pipe. The feeder grabs the animal's neck, pulls the bird close, inserts the pipe down the throat, and initiates pumping. Boiled corn mixed with fat (to aid lubrication) is delivered into the animal via either a fixed number of hand cranks of a mechanical auger or a timed propulsion via a motor. Smaller-scale operations typically use these methods, which fill the animal in about forty-five to sixty seconds. In larger-scale farms, pneumatic devices are preferred, since they can deliver a meal portion in two to three seconds and can be computerized to calculate portions based on the bird's body weight and the size of its previous meal. At the very end of the force-feeding period, the biggest animals receive up to 450 grams of corn at a go. To put this in human perspective, nonprofit personnel in the United States figure on exactly this weight for a single food-bank meal. To put it in goose perspective, premium foie gras livers weigh between 400 and 900 grams. The liver of a normal goose averages 76 grams.

Foie gras fowl, not surprisingly, pant a lot. They also spend much more time sitting than normal ones. Experts differ on whether their overall condition is pathological, meaning diseased (they will recover to a more or less normal state if taken off the force-feeding schedule). Either

way, farmers are careful to get the birds to the slaughter-house after fifteen days or so of force-feeding; otherwise they start dropping dead all on their own.

At the time of this writing, sixteen nations prohibit this form of extreme animal husbandry as inhumane. California's ban will take effect in 2012, and other states are now mulling legislation. Ugly verbal fights have broken out among top chefs over the ethics of rearing foie gras birds, and four-star restaurants serving the stuff in the United States are increasingly the targets of protests.

Foie gras is delicious, especially in the traditional French fashion, cubed atop slices of toasted brioche and washed down with an icy glass of Sauternes. Cookbook writer C. Gerard avows: "The goose is nothing, but man has made of it an instrument for the output of a marvelous product, a kind of living hothouse in which grows the supreme fruit of gastronomy." And so believe many, who consider foie gras one of the most civilized dishes in the world of fine food.

Foo-foo

Foo-foo, a staple dish of central Africa, goes by many names, *fufu*, *foufou*, *ugali*, and *nsima* among them. Its signature component, a ball of pliable starch that sits in a thickened soup, may be made of cassava, yam, plantain, or ground grain. Common to all foo-foo, wherever it is

served, is the way it is eaten. Pinches of the starch are nipped off with the fingers and briefly dragged through the soup. Then the moist morsel is popped in the mouth and swallowed whole, without chewing.

How did this unusual practice come about? Perhaps it is an offshoot of an infant's taking pap from the mother's mouth as the first form of solids. Unable to chew, it swallows the food whole. The warmth with which a Ghanaian speaks of foo-foo leaves no question that it carries great associations of home comfort and caring. Or perhaps foo-foo is swallowed whole for another reason: the lumps amplify the sensation of fullness when other provisions are scarce. Eaten, as it typically is, with beer, foo-foo is a filling dish—one that expands in the stomach like rice or oatmeal. Or maybe there's another reason: foo-foo possibly had its origins as a ritual food and, like the communion wafer, was originally swallowed whole for symbolic reasons.

Getting down to business, foo-foo newcomers find that after the initial, natural hesitation, eating this food is fun. The lump of starch acts like a luge, carrying soupy juices down the throat. Flavored with peanut or palm oil, the soup may also be fiery with peppers. The starch's own flavor is mild. Richard Francis Burton, the famed British explorer, drew a comparison between foo-foo and potatoes: "It is far more savory than that tuber, which has already potatofied at least one nation."

Making foo-foo is an all-afternoon affair. First, the starch source material is boiled. Once it's mushy, it is put into a calf-high wooden container, traditionally carved from a single piece of wood. The person or persons tasked with pounding (there may be as many as three working at

one receptacle) each take a six-foot-tall wooden pestle and begin the long process of converting the starch's glutens into an elastic, springy ball, much as a baker kneads dough. While the pounder thumps the pot, a seated assistant, the turner, makes sure that the mass is constantly turned and the lumps are worked out. The process is unhurried; getting the starch table-ready can take an hour. Despite the easy pace, accidental mashing is an occupational hazard for the turner's fingers. Singing is a time-honored way for participants to maintain a steady rhythm and stave off accidents.

If you have been honored by an invitation to eat foo-foo, several things are helpful to know. First, you must wash your hands before dinner, which of course you always do, but now it's extra important since you use your fingers to eat and there's a communal bowl. Soap and water may be provided at the table for this purpose. Second, you always eat foo-foo with your right hand, even if you're a lefty, because the left hand is traditionally used for other hygienic matters. Third, the all-important starch-snipping action takes practice to get right. You first moisten your fingers in a second bowl of nonsoapy water that will be placed on the table. Then set the tips of your index and middle fingers down in the soup at the edge of the foo-foo. Yes, down in the soup. Pivoting the fingers around, scissor off a nip of dough, using your thumb to help pluck it away. Next drag it through the soup, and quickly put it into your mouth.

Here, stresses David Mohammed, owner of the Akra Sima restaurant in south London, tidiness is the ideal. "You want to eat the foo-foo cleanly," he advises. "You don't want it to look like the chickens have been at it."

Keeping your fingers moist with soup or water will help with the dough, as will a methodical approach, working from the perimeter inward. To swallow the lump, work it to the back of your tongue, relax your throat, and let the natural action of your swallowing muscles carry it down. This will feel strange at first (though possibly less so to some than to others). With a good African beer to hand (try Star, Club, Gulder, or Ngoma lager), you'll get the hang of it.

Fresh Blood

Sheltered as we Americans are from the gory realities of the slaughterhouse, many of us flinch at the mere sight of blood. Its shock value stems both from its red-alert hue and from its nature as a life force that is ordinarily hidden. There are few things more vital than blood as it spills, and few things more stagnant than a fly-ridden, gory puddle.

Is it a coincidence that the popular rise of vampire stories coincided with the industrialization of animal butchering, and the sequestering of childbearing women and accident victims into hospitals? As blood became less and less commonplace, it took on a legendary life as the preferred food of monsters—monsters who, like blood itself, wasted upon exposure to the light of day.

Yet there are still places and situations in the world where eating blood (like mother's milk, blood is more food than drink) is unremarkable. Once cooked, it frequently finds a place at the European and Asian table in the form of blood sausage (variously known as blood pudding, *blutwurst*, *boudin noir*, or *morcilla*). Recipes call for diverse combinations of blood, meat, fat, and filler, or the sausage can be simpler, more spartan fare, as described in Homer's *Odyssey*: "When a man besides a great fire has filled a sausage with fat and blood and turns it this way and that and is very eager to get it quickly roasted . . ."

The ancient Romans also had a taste for blood, in their cooking and in their entertainment. In the name of self-healing, some individuals managed to combine the two interests. As Pliny reports in his *Natural History*, "epileptic patients are in the habit of drinking the blood even of gladiators, draughts teeming with life, as it were; a thing when we see it done by wild beasts entering upon the same arena, inspires us with horror at the spectacle! And yet these persons forsooth consider it a most effectual cure for their disease, to quaff the warm, breathing blood from man himself, and, as they apply their mouth to the wound, to draw forth his very life."

At least the epileptics had a medical excuse for this macabre pursuit; in a still more decadent vein, able-bodied Roman nobles were also said to indulge, simply for the instant transfusion of gladiatorial essence. Today, with human blood off the menu (barring psychopaths and paper-cut soothers), individuals hoping for a shot of red courage will go to an animal source. Freshly slaughtered bull's blood is available at market abattoirs in Colombia, among other countries, and in Taipei's Snake Alley you can get a shot of cobra blood with the reptile's still-pulsing heart as a chaser.

The festival of Deodhani in Kamakhya, India, is another place where animal blood is consumed in the raw. If you happen to visit, give loudly shrieking devotees a lot of room, for they believe themselves to be temporary incarnations of the cruelest, most vengeful deities in the Hindu pantheon. As the celebration progresses, the godly side eclipses the human. Some of the gods, especially Kali, are very, very bloodthirsty. Near the festival's climax, devotees will bite the heads off pigeons, Ozzy-style, and drink down the gushing flow.

On the flanks of Mount Kilimanjaro, fresh blood is consumed not as an ecstatic release from mortal life, but as a means to sustain it. The Maasai people and their kindred tribe, the Samburu, have historically been pastoralists, raising cattle, sheep, goats, and camels. In former times they lived largely off the products of these animals, with cattle blood being an important source of renewable protein when milk production declined at the end of the rainy season. Animals would be bled at the neck with a tourniquet and a stubby arrow, yielding enough blood to be caught in a gourd container. The wound would be stopped with mud or dung, and the beast left alone for a month or so to replenish.

The routine, outpatient nature of this procedure has a more dramatic counterpart—the drinking of an animal's blood in the course of its slaughter. Here, blood gains a more powerful aura, as it comes at the cost of the animal's life. Traditional cooking expert William Rubel, author of *The Magic of Fire*, lived among the Samburu. Here he describes the suffocation and subsequent bloodletting of a sheep at the end of a long day's walk:

We were up near Maralal. Once I understood that we were going to slaughter a sheep, I offered my knife—a razor-sharp French Opinel knife. I always provide my knife for slaughters when I see that the one being proposed for the slaughter is not as sharp as mine. The sheep was turned on its back. . . . My friend John, who has subsequently died of AIDS, held the sheep's head so that he could keep its mouth shut and close its nostrils. When the sheep passed out my knife was used to skin the sheep over the heart—a piece of skin was cut in an arc and pulled back to form a pocket. The sheep's heart was stabbed with the knife and its blood pumped into the pocket formed by this skin. Each of us bent over the sheep; we each put our mouth down into the blood and drank. I drank last, and as I drank a great gush of oxygen was pumped out of the heart—causing the blood to foam pink. I had had no expectations regarding the taste—if asked, I would probably have said that I'd expect the blood to taste salty, or metallic. In fact, the blood tasted fresh, delightfully fresh. That was my feeling at the time— refreshing. I had walked several miles that day—hadn't eaten much—and so was probably both a little thirsty and a little hungry.

A transfusion: immediate, essential, and needles are beside the point.

Frog's Leg

☹ 🐸

How did a certain nationality get its nickname? A couple theories are kicking around, but the most likely answer is the Gallic appetite for frog's legs. One estimate reckons that the French populace consumes *cuisses de grenouilles* with such avarice that twenty thousand frogs per year are sacrificed to the cause.

The French aren't the only diners with a taste for things that go hop in the night. Historically, most of Europe enjoyed the delicate white meat. It was especially popular during Lent, when chicken, cows, and pigs were forbidden to Christians, but the church looked the other way when it came to amphibians. The only European country where the creature didn't catch on was in England, where the term "frog" for Frenchmen is still gleefully applied (the French counterstrike by calling Brits *les rosbifs*).

For a time, frog's legs were the daily special in the United States too. During the California gold rush, they were consumed on a massive scale. As James P. Collins relates in an article for *Natural History* magazine, prospectors poured into the state in search of an instant fortune. They came in such numbers that the larders of food provisioners often became bare, so the provisioners turned to the ponds. During the peak harvest of 1895, some 120,000 frogs met their end in the pan.

A portion of the world's supply of edible frogs is farmed, notably in Taiwan, China, Vietnam, and Indonesia—all countries where frog is eaten on a regular basis. Frog farming is a positive development, because, as Collins's article details, many species are in steep decline, in part due to over hunting, and in part due to factors like global warming, urban encroachment into formerly wild areas, and toxic chemicals.

While Asian frog farmers seem to be making a go of it, rearing the animals is a difficult venture. Among the hassle factors are the two-year development time from tadpole to bullfrog, and the fact that frogs don't like food that doesn't move. To solve the latter problem, Japanese researchers brainstormed a delivery system in which dead silkworm pupae roll around on motorized trays. All well and good for the committed frog farmer, but for the average get-rich-quick wannabe with a swampy acre to spare, the whole business is more fraught with uncertainty.

This means most of the world's supply of edible frog's legs are still hunted from the wild. In the United States, especially in the wetland regions of the South and Southeast, the quarry is usually the bullfrog, a (nonendangered) species that's the granddaddy of all frogs, growing as big as seven pounds and up to a foot and a half in length. The hunting method is called gigging. Gigging is a rich subculture unto itself, complete with generations' worth of wisdom on tools and technique.

The standard equipment for frog gigging includes two men and a boat. This can be either a canoe or a flat-bottomed vessel, which, if power-driven, is equipped with a near-silent motor. The hunters arm themselves with a Maglite or headlamp, a net, a frog sack, and a gig, which is a trident-shaped fork with razor-sharp tines firmly attached to a long pole, either commercially made or rigged to a bamboo stalk or a broom handle. Optional equipment includes a small bat and/or rifle. Come nightfall, the giggers hit tidewater channels at low tide, when the frogs tend to gather on the banks. As quietly as possible, following the distinctive *rubba-thump* croak of the full-sized male frog, the boat is maneuvered close to the shore (it is possible to gig on foot, but the vibrations on the ground give the frogs an advantage). Once a target is sighted, the flashlight is snapped into the creature's eyes, which momentarily dazzles it. The moment of truth: the gigger plunges the tines into the frog, aiming to run it through and pinion it into the mud. With a swift sweep of the net, the frog is bagged. At this point the bat is a handy helper for those stubborn animals that refuse to succumb to the gig's tines. The .22 is employed when frogs are out of gigging range. Note to would-be giggers: In most states a hunting or fishing license is required to take frogs from waters, and some states prohibit the use of firearms, artificial lights, and explosives—check your local regulations.

The reward for the gigger is the freshest of frog legs, enjoyed sautéed in oil over an open fire. As a general practice, the frog is skinned. To do this, you make an incision on the back of the animal just below the head, take a (clean) pair of pliers and pull the back skin straight downward off the legs, then flip the animal over and reverse the procedure. (In Laos, frog skin is enjoyed in its own right, deep-fried until it is crackling crisp. Once cooked, it resembles a large piece of speckled pork rind with small shriveled legs. Its taste is likewise similar to pork rind, with an almost imperceptible hint of aquarium scum. It is served with a chili–rice vinegar dip.) After discarding the head of the now-skinned frog, you gut it, remove its hands and feet, and give it a good wash, whereupon it is ready for the frying pan.

Frog's legs are a completely inoffensive fine-grained meat, universally likened to chicken. Once they're prepared for the table, the most off-putting thing about them is their resemblance to well-muscled human legs. The great chef Escoffier, working at the Carlton Hotel, managed to turn this to his advantage when he cooked them for the notoriously randy Prince of Wales. He called them *cuisses de nymphes aurore* (legs of the dawn nymphs). In circumstances considerably less posh, out in the American wetlands, giggers will fry themselves up a pair or two at daybreak, reward for a hard night's chase. Even though they're sitting in a swamp instead of a fancy dining room, they know what it's like to eat like a prince.

Fugu

If it has all gone very badly wrong, the symptoms begin ten to forty-five minutes after your first bite. First your lips tingle, then they go numb. Next you feel light-headed and dizzy and experience feelings of impending doom. Finally, when the poison blocks your nerve transmissions completely, paralysis sets in from the feet up. Unless drastic emergency measures are taken, you die, fully conscious until asphyxiation from dead lungs drags you under.

Then there's the less attractive scenario. The toxin seeps through your system and you're fully aware of your plight, but it's not quite enough to finish you off. You can't move a single muscle, not a twitch or a flicker. In which case you get buried alive.

Known as *fugu* in Japan, the blowfish of the genuses *Fugu* and *Sphoeroides* deflates Japan's population by fifty or so individuals every year. The toxin is 1,250 times deadlier than cyanide, and the royal family is forbidden by decree from eating the fish. This is the ultimate extreme food, the one exotic dish most gourmands can pass up. Yet the Japanese, and increasingly diners in Hong Kong and New York, are eating heaps of the stuff.

If you choose to eat fugu in Japan, you literally put your life in the hands of the restaurant's chef, a highly trained and licensed professional whose job it is to remove the eleven poison-rich parts of the fish, including the liver, ovaries, skin, and skeleton. This is a man who keeps his knife very sharp—keener by far than ordinary sashimi blades. A lethal amount of toxin, one or two milligrams, could fit in the dot on this *i*. As good as he is, there's always the chance a chef might have a bad night, which has always been part of the fugu mystique. As one sixteenth-century poet wrote: "Last night I ate fugu with a friend. Today I helped carry his coffin." In certain regions of Japan, they don't act so hastily. If someone goes rigid after eating fugu, their body isn't buried for three days. If it doesn't start to smell, they conclude that the poor stiff is still in there, and hope there's a chance he'll recover. Even safely prepared fish may bring a mild tingle to the sides of the tongue and lips—for fugu lovers, a fleeting kiss with death that only adds to the pleasure. Some say that in these microscopic doses, the toxin is addictive, another explanation for its allure.

If you eat fugu in the United States, however, you are eating, according to the man who oversees its import, "the safest fish in America." Nobuyoshi Kuraoka, president of the Wako International USA Trading Company, is being funny, but he isn't joking. He has managed to overcome the seemingly impossible hurdle of FDA regulation against deadly restaurant entrees by ensuring that his blowfish are as harmless as Hello Kitty. The process begins at the fish warehouses at the port of Shimonoseki in Japan, the clearinghouse of 80 percent of the world's edible puffers, or blowfish. Here master fugu chefs with twenty years' experience clean and filet Kuraoka's U.S.-bound *torafugu*, or tiger blowfish, the only species allowed into our country. Its skin, with its distinctive markings, is left on to verify that the fish is not an imposter. The filets are then further tested by Shimonoseki market inspectors for the presence of the teterodoxin poison. Once they are cleared by the inspectors, they're packed in ice in specially sealed boxes and shipped via JAL flight 6016 to New York's Kennedy Airport. Mr. Kuraoka meets this thrice-yearly delivery at the airport with an FDA inspector, and if the shipment meets the approval of all, it is sent on to parts elsewhere.

All fugu is not created equal in the toxicity department. According to the fugu chef at Tokyo's Kuromonto restaurant, two kinds of blowfish are ushered through the Shimonoseki market. The first is caught from the wild during the season that runs from October through March. It will kill with authority if it is improperly prepared. The second kind is farmed, and the risk of toxicity, says the chef, is reduced (though still potentially present) because the fish does not consume as much of the ocean-going bacteria that are thought to be the building blocks of the poison. The farmed variety predominates in Japanese fugu restaurants. A full seven-course fugu dinner in Tokyo can cost as much as two hundred dollars. Diners in that country who are specifically seeking dinner-as-death-threat may want to check on their fish's origins to ensure that they're getting their full money's worth.

The Japanese authorities make no distinction between wild and farmed fish when it comes to the licensing of fugu chefs. No matter what they're carving, all are expected to complete a two-year course of study, and, in Tokyo, pass annual competency exams (the specific regulations differ from region to region). Only 40 percent of aspiring chefs who take the test pass it, so it is truly the top guns (or top *fugu-hiki* knives) that are overseeing your dinner.

Health and safety are obviously paramount in fugu preparation, but another component factors in its high price. With its presentation, the artistry of the kitchen, its ability to assemble beauty and flavor in multiple variations on a fishy theme, is tested to the ultimate. For it's not just a death wish that drives people to eat this particular sea creature. Many also consider it the most delicious of all fishes, with a delicate, elusive flavor and a pleasing elasticity in the mouth.

If you are fortunate enough to take part in a multi-course fugu dinner in Japan, here is what you might expect:

The meal traditionally begins with a fugu-flavored cocktail made with sake and toasted fins, one of which bobs on the top. Its taste is unusual—rice wine rich in omega-3s—and the hot version is better than the cold. It sets the tone for the first plate of fugu sashimi, beautifully arranged in the form of a chrysanthemum, sliced so thin that the plate's elaborate decoration is visible below. Small mounds of daikon radish and red pepper are presented on a separate dish—some of this should be mixed into your bowl of soy sauce, the remainder put atop the fish slices, which are then rolled into packets, dipped in the sauce, and eaten. Pace yourself with the food and the sake, for there's plenty more to come. Perhaps grilled fugu, which looks innocuous on the brazier, as innocent as a halibut steak. But this is wild fish that you're eating in Kuromonto, and until the day before yesterday it was packed to the gills with poison. The waitress next presents a plate of shredded fugu skin, which comes as a surprise, since you thought this was one of the fugu offcuts that gets sealed in a special locked barrel and burned as hazardous waste. But apparently not. At this point—you must be imagining it—you're beginning to lose sensation on the sides of your tongue. Or maybe it's for real: a skilled fugu chef can leave just enough poison on the parts that he's serving to mess with the nerve endings of his clients. Things are getting a bit hazy and deconstructed at this point, time to slow down with the sake. The next course appears to be a one-pot dish made with fugu and various vegetables. You're finding it hard to focus on exactly what they are because you've just lost all sensation in your hands. You can move them, you just can't *feel* them. What's that about? And you're definitely feeling sensations of impending doom—one of the warning signs all the articles talk about. As you frantically jiggle your hands under the table, the final course is served, a porridgy rice dish made with any leftovers. With icy, quaking fingers, you manage a couple bites.

As you stare bleakly at the fine blond grain of the wood of your table, watching it take on life of its own, you rue the now-inevitable ebb of yours. The waitress brightly offers a special treat, found only in select fugu restaurants and appreciated only by true connoisseurs. Wanly, you try to pay attention. The ovaries of the puffer fish. The generative organs that will seal the deal, turning your too too-solid flesh into a custom-fit coffin. She says the ovaries have been pickled in salt and rice wine sediment for three years, which affords enough time for all the poison to break down. Why not, you're going to die anyway. You pick at the sour grainy substance, knowing that you've just swallowed the most deadly parts of a very deadly animal, and somewhere this counts for something. But the situation shows signs of improvement. While dicing with death over the ovaries, sensation has returned to your hands. It must have been the sake after all. Or else the chef really is a sadistic genius with his fugu-hiki blade.

When it comes to eating fugu and enjoying the experience, the best advice is to pick your restaurant very carefully, and know exactly what you're eating. One more piece of advice—even if you're not very adept with them, try not to drop your chopsticks during dinner. This is a telltale sign of spreading paralysis, and the staff is liable to take it personally.

Gelatin Shot

Once upon a time, there was a college brew known as Jungle Juice. It consisted of a couple fifths of cheap alcohol, a few quarts of mixers, and green Gatorade snuck from the varsity fridge. The time-honored serving vessel was a garbage can, which, in the best-case scenario, had been hosed out by the social chairman before the Jungle Juice was mixed. Then came the 1990s. Good-bye Rubbermaid, hello Dixie. The gelatin shot was born, along with a whole new way of getting shitfaced. There was only one problem. Even today, a decade and a half later, few people can do a gelatin shot without looking stupid. A different kind of stupid from drinking out of a garbage can, but stupid all the same.

An aside on terminology: According to the definitive book on the subject, *Jiggelo: Inventive Gelatin Shots for Creative Imbibers*, "do" is indeed the correct action verb to describe the downing of a gelatin shot. According to the authors, "you don't sip it, you chew it. You don't drink it, you do it."

As befits a cocktail composed largely of gelatin, the original inventors are hard to pin down. Singer-satirist Tom Lehrer takes personal credit, saying he invented the shot while he was in the army in the 1950s, as a way of bypassing the base's ban on alcoholic beverages. But the idea didn't go wide until much later—possibly propagated by bored homemakers, or some guys in a chemistry lab who prioritized getting blotto over winning the Nobel, or even the government (Nixon to Hoover: "The LSD didn't work, maybe this'll get those goddamn hippies off the street"). However it happened, once it built some momentum, the gelatin shot spread like a nasty stain in frat-house party rooms across the land.

Potent and yet wiggly. There's something incongruous about that. And something equally incongruous about a three-hundred-pound all-state linebacker holding that teeny-weeny plastic or paper cup in his hand. It looks like the meds container they dole out at bedtime at the mental unit. Moreover, the gelatin shot, unlike the liquid variety, can't be manfully knocked back. Gelatin clumps; that's its defining property. If it's thrown faceward, it goes splat in the eye, or on the anterior wall. Likewise, once a gelatin shot is consumed, the empty container can't be slammed decisively down on the bar. Stubbing a toe hurts. Stubbing a whole hand hurts more.

So what *is* the best way to do a gelatin shot? In *Jiggelo*, the authors list the various methods that mankind—in the grand tradition of Pythagoras, da Vinci, and the Wright brothers—has devised to dislodge the shot from the cup. These include:

1. Using a spoon to scoop it out

2. Using a spoon, finger, or tongue to detach the gelatin from the inner surface of the cup so it can be tipped into the mouth and swallowed

3. Squeezing the container's contents into the mouth (works with paper, not plastic)

4. Using fingers and/or teeth to rip the container apart (ditto)

If you have a tongue like a calf's, or that guy from Kiss, using it to free the gelatin is certainly the most effective way to attract the attention and interest of those nearby. A more subtle approach is finger-rimming, which has the benefits of being quick and discreet and has seduction value in that you can lick your fingertip clean. The remaining methods do not merit discussion, except to say that spoons are perfectly acceptable with dessert shots (for example the nummy-sounding crème brûlée recipe *Jiggelo* provides on page 74).

Speaking of calves, theirs is the sacrifice that makes your hangover possible. Or pigs, poultry, or fish. Gelatin can be made from either bones or skin. Defleshed and degreased bones are crushed and treated with weak acid to extract the protein, which is then processed into a finely milled powder. Animal hide (or fish skin, if kosher gelatin is sought) is subjected to a similar collagen-releasing bath lasting from one day to several weeks, depending on the species and age of the animal. Gelatin is, essentially, the glue that holds skin and bones together.

While the gelatin shot phenomenon seems to offer a major opportunity for manufacturers to capitalize on a judgment-impaired, youthful market, fear of corrupting actual minors appears to have won the day. Nowhere on the Kraft Foods website is there any mention of the Jell-O shot, even though this is the most widely used, if trademark-infringing, name of the item.

More emphatically, legislators in the state of Connecticut—*so* not getting it—attempted to ban the sale of gelatin shots in bars, fearing that the medium disguised the taste of alcohol all too effectively and ingestors could easily have one too many. The proposed ban never made it into law; gelatin shots are still being done in Connecticut. All to the good, according to the information disseminated in the brochure "All About Gelatine," put out by the Gelatine Manufacturers of Europe:

Gelatine has a positive effect on the bones, cartilage, tendons, and ligaments. Reputable dieticians and doctors recommend a dose of 10g of gelatin a day as an optimum intake. . . . Gelatine also strengthens the connective tissue, thus ensuring firm skin, shiny hair and strong fingernails. It has been proved that hydration of the skin is boosted by consuming gelatin. This has the positive consequence that wrinkles become less deep and the skin looks firmer and fresher.

Points to take away: gelatin shots are tasty, they get you blitzed, they get you some action (if you have a tongue like a calf's), and they may actually *make you look younger*. Especially for all the baby boomers who were forced to drink their alcohol out of a garbage can, these are excuses you can run with.

Geoduck Clam

First, a word about the strange pronunciation of "geo-duck" (goo-ee-duck). The Nisqualli people, native to the Pacific Northwest, gave the clam a name that sounds like "gwe-duck," which in their language meant "dig deep." Back east, a dictionary editor who was compiling new words from the western territories jumbled the letters. His version became the official way to spell it, while the Nisqualli pronunciation remained approximately the same. The upshot is, the clam is correctly called "gooey." If this is too complicated, you can simply call it "the obscene-looking giant one." People who know geoducks will know what you mean.

Now on to its hunt and capture. Never mind bull running in Pamplona or whale chasing off the Newfoundland coast. In the annals of man versus beast, there are few competitions as frenzied, as taxing, and as muddy as that of man versus geoduck clam.

Apart from discerning shellfish fans, few people living beyond the northwest coast of the United States and western Canada have even heard of this bivalve mollusk. Its reputation ought to be bigger, if only for its appearance. It is the largest burrowing clam in the world, averaging three pounds but reaching upward of ten, with soft parts measuring over a meter long. It gets so big because it lives a long time—over one hundred years' worth of growth rings have been counted on the shell of one senior member.

The animal's appearance is distinctive thanks to its siphon, a wrinkly, flexible, highly extendable appendage through which the clam takes in and then blows clear oxygenated water and plankton. Once a mature clam has settled down in its permanent home, about three feet below the mud of the seabed, its siphon stretches upward and emerges just past the sandy silt into the water. The siphon can be up to thirty-nine inches, as long as an arm. Should the clam need to suddenly make itself small, it's got a problem. The siphon is too big for its britches, and even in its most compact state lolls ungainly and flaccid out of the shell. For diners in the Far East, this trait alone vaults the gooey into the aphrodisiac all-stars. But then the clam tops itself with the showstopping gimmick of squirting a high-pressure jet of salt water onto unsuspecting bystanders, followed by some dribbly ooze.

It is especially prone to squirting when it's being hunted, probably out of shock, because basically all the animal wants is a quiet life. Naturalists venture that it lives so long because it has few natural predators and a couch-potato lifestyle, never moving from its sandy bunker unless a freak storm or a geoduck clammer happens to dislodge it.

Professional geoduck hunters work underwater, equipped with diving gear and water jets to blast the animals into the open. Amateurs work on the flats at low tide, their equipment a clamming sleeve, shovel, and determination. Upon spying the small ringed mound that indicates a gooey down below, the clammer launches into a frenzy of digging with the shovel, until the hole is about two feet deep. At this point the sleeve—a DIY plastic ring about a foot or two high and shoulder-width in diameter— is stuck firmly into the hole to keep the sand walls from falling in on themselves. Feverishly, the digging starts anew, perhaps now with a spade, or a clam shell, or clenched fingers rubbed raw by the cold coarse sand. The digger is upside down to the shoulders in a dark, sloshy hole, knees joining the fingers in the scraped-raw department. But he can't slow down, because the trophy is now but inches away. At this point the clammer starts feeling around for the largely-retracted-but-still-ridiculously-huge siphon. Finding it, the clammer uses it as a kind of towrope to locate the animal's shell. Geoduck experts warn against pulling the animal out by its clamhood, for fear of grave injury (to the mollusk). With the prize in the fingertips, it is up to the clammer to push, pull, and wrest the shell from its stronghold. With a mighty yank, the job is done. Man and beast emerge to low whistles of admiration, the clam for its meat, the clammer for his dogged motion, which frequently wins the day, but not always.

Once the animal has been shucked from its shell with a sharp paring knife (the siphon and a small crescent of meat below are the edible parts), it is necessary to strip off the tough outer skin. To do this, you hold the siphon under hot water; the skin will begin to separate from the layer below. After peeling off the skin, you wash the siphon thoroughly and split lengthwise. Next you cut it crosswise into paper-thin slices. It's now ready to cook, as quickly as possible (to avoid its toughening) in a broth, chowder, or stir-fry. The meat will be pleasantly chewy and unbelievably sweet, like a good scallop. If hunting one down is out of the question and you're not in the Northwest, you may find gooey in a good sushi restaurant, where it goes by the name of *murugai*, or giant clam.

Giant Waterbug

The creature is horrible, easily as long as your thumb. It has jagged spindly legs and mandibles that can puncture and suck dry a frog. The tiny strip of red binding that trusses its legs only underlines its fondest wish to skitter straight onto your scalp. It and its ten fellows on the teal-green glazed plate in the Warorot market in Chiang Mai, Thailand, look just like the bouncer-sized cockroaches that infest metropolitan areas. But, in fact, they are distantly related creatures of the water, at home in the puddles, paddies, and ponds across Southeast Asia.

The specimens on the plate are males of the species *Lethocerus indicus*, which are pricier than their female counterparts due to a special pheromone they exude from glands near the anus. This sexual attractant—which has an intense flowery flavor/aroma reminiscent of hyacinth or pear—is of course deeply attractive to lady waterbugs. Less expectedly, it has a near-Proustian appeal for the Vietnamese people, who use precious droplets of the essence in their cooking. Vials of the essence, called *ca cuang*, were once available (if expensive) in the markets in Hanoi. Nowadays it's difficult to find—a nectar spirited away by emigrants, either for their own use or to sell for a king's ransom to others. A synthetic version made from hexanol esters roughly mimics the pheromone's spicy pear scent. While the substitute is good enough to find ongoing buyers in Asian food stores, it makes authentic ca cuang lovers shudder and pine for the old days.

Back in Thailand, waterbug affairs are more rough-and-ready, beginning with the creature's common name, *mangda* or *maengda*, which also means "pimp." (*Mangdana* is yet another variant.) In this country, the male bugs are also used as a flavoring component, but instead of being milked for the pure essence, the bugs are crushed to a pulp in a mortar, along with chiles, garlic, shallots, sugar, fish sauce, and other flavorings, to make one of the many delectable versions of *nam prik* paste. The female bugs are also consumed, battered and deep-fried, out of hand.

A very thick carapace armors the bug, much of which—the head; the hard exterior wing casing; the fragile, oil-soaked tissuey wings; and the legs—needs to be plucked, pulled, or broken away before the rest can be eaten. The fully stripped bug is slightly less intimidating (because it's smaller and less obviously a bug), but the near-translucent belly still requires nerve to bite into. The sensation of doing so is primitive—it's you versus the creepy-crawly, and you're going to win. Once you've bitten down, you realize that you've tasted something similar before—soft-shell crab. Which, between the chitinous exterior and arthropod guts—spiny bits and mushy bits—shares more than a few gene strings in common with the lady *Lethocerus*. While experienced maengda eaters with formidable mandibles of their own might be able to handle all the roughage, you might find yourself spitting out the chewed carcass in a greenish, fibrous mass.

It's improbable that, like older Vietnamese, you'll find yourself dreaming wistfully of giant waterbug essence once you've had the real thing between your teeth. But the experience of eating it is a good one. It didn't kill you. Since there are twenty grams of protein per hundred grams of maengda, it did indeed make you stronger.

Guinea Pig

☹ ⊙ 🐓

Archaeological evidence shows that the people of the Andean high plains regions of southern Peru and Bolivia have been eating domesticated guinea pig since about 5000 BC. Word has just filtered through to Lovemyguinea .com, to the stunned disbelief of the chat forum:

Those people are beasts! This is utter horror. How can anybody eat one of the adorable kissy-nose darlings?!!

It's the kind of outrage that always arises when people who adore animals dearly encounter people who adore the same animals with hot sauce. But that's how things are in Peru, Ecuador, Bolivia, and Colombia, where guinea pigs are small, furry, kissy-nosed livestock.

While increasingly farmed on a commercial scale for table consumption, in rural regions they are still kept in household kitchens, running free, feeding on alfalfa and table scraps, bedding down in the evening in little adobe hutches called *cuyeros* (*cuy* being the local name for the animal). While a home-reared cuy might be given a name, like a yard chicken, it is not typical practice. Children are the chief caretakers, cleaning the floor and the hutches, and possibly owning an animal or two out of the typical household herd of about twenty head, an allowance and 4-H project in one runty package.

Cuy have a longstanding role in traditional medicine. A healer will pass an animal over the body of an afflicted patient, after which it is sacrificed so the illness can be divined from the entrails. Mostly, though, the animals are sacrificed for the table, especially for festive dinners. Regional variations abound: after skinning and gutting, the cuy might be cut up and braised in a stew, fried in pepper sauce, boiled in a soup, or served as it is in Cuzco, spit-roasted with head, paws, and tail intact, until it is crackling golden, much like a small suckling pig with a ratty demeanor and a chile pepper in its mouth instead of an apple.

Prepared in this way, cuy is eaten with the fingers, leaving a distinctive sweet, smoky smell on the fingertips that locals call *tufo*. The meat runs close to the many small bones and is said to taste like rabbit or chicken. A standard accompaniment is beer or *chicha,* a lightly alcoholic corn-based beverage first distilled by the Incas.

As difficult as it can be for nonnatives to reconcile the notions of adorably squeaking pet and cuy fried Huanuco-style, the little animal is embedded in Peruvian culture as forkworthy. Nowhere is this more clear than in the Cuzco cathedral, where, in an eighteenth-century painting by Marcos Zapata, Jesus and the disciples are seated at the table for the Last Supper. Plated before them is not the traditional lamb, but, given away by its paws and buck teeth, a roasted guinea pig.

Hákarl

Come the last week of January in Iceland, this small island country in the middle of the North Atlantic unites in the monthlong celebration known as Thorrablot, a hearkening back to the exploits of the land's Viking ancestry. These weeks are marked by traditional games, the singing of old Icelandic songs, heavy drinking, and above all the eating of the traditional foods of the bygone days, when longships ruled the seas and terrified the shores.

While the Vikings did have wicked swords and helmets, they lacked artificial preservatives. Most of the foods they ate were either dried, pickled in whey, salted, or smoked. Among the delicacies eaten come Thorrablottime are twice-cooked sheeps' heads (first charred black, then boiled) and pickled rams' testicles. But even these Valhalla-caliber goodies shrivel in comparison with the platters of *hákarl*, cubed pieces of meat whose bite-sized proportions and tawny pink coloring may give a falsely benign first impression. Essentially, hákarl (now to be revealed as putrefied shark meat) does to your taste buds what Viking marauders once did to unsuspecting Scottish villages of yore.

It's strange but true: only the deliberate invitation of rot makes the meat edible at all. In its fresh state, the flesh of the North Atlantic–native Greenland shark is toxic, causing symptoms ranging from mild stupor (for their part, Greenlanders call drunkenness being "shark-sick") to death. The main culprit appears to be high levels of an organic chemical called trimethylamine oxide, which is in the flesh to help neutralize the shark's equally high levels of urea, a by-product of protein metabolism that humans quickly excrete via urine.

Long ago, an Icelandic householder discovered that by burying shark meat deep in beach gravel for two to three months, the poisonous elements began to leach out. Not the smell, though, an eye-stinging combination of bad fish, stale urine, and ammonia that survives even the second stage of hákarl preparation: wind-drying in a drafty shack for another two to four months. Once the meat has stopped leaking and is more or less firm, it is ready for the celebrants of Thorrablot.

These sons and daughters of the god of thunder wouldn't think of eating hákarl without a shot of ice-cold *brennavín*, a potato-based liquor whose eighty-proof alcohol content helps finish off any pathogens still seething in the fish, and whose caraway seed flavoring in no way masks hákarl breath later on.

Few people seem to relish hákarl, even the Icelanders who grew up on it. And if you give it some thought, other things begin to make sense. With dishes like this at home—along with the sheeps' heads and testicles—you can understand why the Vikings were so dead-set on travel abroad.

Honeycomb

Since man and bee have been keeping each other company long before recorded history began, our civilization is replete with honeycomb lore. One often-repeated beekeeping legend is that a honeycomb discovered in an ancient Egyptian tomb was still edible (if a tad dusty) many thousands of years later. This is not entirely far-fetched.

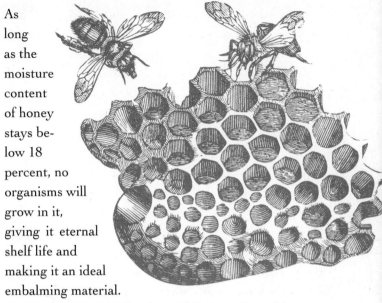

As long as the moisture content of honey stays below 18 percent, no organisms will grow in it, giving it eternal shelf life and making it an ideal embalming material.

More romantically, the yielding quality of beeswax and the utter sweetness of its contents inspired the poet of the Song of Solomon: "I am come into my garden, my sister, [my] spouse: I have gathered my myrrh with my spice; I have eaten my honeycomb with my honey; I have drunk my wine with my milk: eat O friends; drink yea, drink abundantly, O beloved." Later on in the Bible, following Jesus's resurrection and reappearance to his disciples on earth, Christ dined on honeycomb and broiled fish at the supper at Emmaus, proving himself to be a man, not a ghost.

Eternal life, consuming pleasures, mortality: honeycomb is rich with allusions to the basic nature of being, but it is one of those exceptional foods that has never had life of its own. Instead it is shelter, an intricate construction of hexagonal, waxen cells that make up the hive in which the honeybees dwell. The wax itself is made with honey as a raw material. It is produced by wax-making bees, specialized teams of workers that gang together to construct the comb's new partitions. A worker gorges on honey, which is converted in its body into beeswax, which is secreted from eight wax glands on the abdomen. It emerges as a liquid but soon hardens into a strong yet flexible storage unit for honey and immature bees.

Within the hive, the comb takes on different roles according to its location. The lower levels act as incubation chambers for baby bees. Farther up along the side walls is the honey storage area—where the hexagonal cubbies hold the food energy that nourishes the young and powers the old. Honey is made when a worker bee gathers nectar from local flowers and stores it in a specialized organ called a honey stomach, which has a capacity of seventy milligrams. The bee regurgitates and swallows the honey several times, mixing it with enzymes that will prevent the nectar's sugars from fermenting. After about half an hour the honey is regurgitated for the last time into the cells. Bees then fan it with their wings to evaporate residual water to less than 20 percent, leaving the sticky substance we love. Bees love it too; a hive typically produces two to three times more than is necessary for the colony's survival, which is why we're able to take it from them without great disruption to the hive's function.

Today, practitioners of natural medicine advise people suffering from plant allergies to chew a bit of locally produced honeycomb every day for a month before hay fever season, in the belief that the pollen molecules it contains will help immunize the eater against the airborne ones to follow (when a bee takes nectar from a flower, pollen sticks to its legs and ends up in the honeycomb). People also chew beeswax recreationally, like gum, and purposely seek out comb honey, which comes with a chunk of beeswax in the container. Since the wax passes harmlessly through the digestive system, some chewers go ahead and swallow the comb once its sweet goodness is extracted; others spit it out. Either way the wax tends to stick to the teeth.

The best place to buy comb honey is from a local beekeeper or health food store. There is no need to worry about unpleasant larval surprises. In domesticated hives, the egg-laying queen is separated from the honey-bearing top levels by an excluder, which keeps the queen and the brood segregated from the portions that will be jarred.

Honeycomb is no longer considered a luxury food, but it ought to be, by virtue of its deliciousness, and the fact that it was once fit for ancient princes—among them the earthly poet of the Song of Solomon, an Egyptian bound for the afterlife, and Jesus, who was just stopping through.

Honeypot Ant

Digging for honeypot ants is hot, dusty work. Under the Australian outback's broiling sun, the only source of shade is the sparse stand of mulga trees under which the ants build their underground chambers. M. Hart, cited in

Gene DeFoliart's online book, *The Human Use of Insects as a Food Resource*, describes an excavation by a group of Aboriginal women:

They looked for the black ants on the ground, followed them to their almost invisible holes and then the women dug down with wana, *the sharp digging sticks, scooping the earth out with the* piti, *the carrying dishes. The children watched every move intently as the women dug deep down, the perspiration streaming from their foreheads.*

Presently the digging in one hole stopped, the woman reached for the carrying dish, and shook out the dust, and the children leaned dangerously forward over the six-foot-deep pit. The mother loosened a couple of clods of earth and pulled out a handful of the strange looking ants, showing their transparent abdomens extended with golden honey to the size of small marbles. She straightened up, passed the carrying dish up to the oldest child and watched as the five-year-old boy put the ball into his mouth, sucked out the honey and threw the ant away. He passed the dish on to the next child and they shared the honey-ants around.

Before sweeteners were an everyday commodity, honeypot ants—native to desert and semiarid regions in Australia, Africa, and North and South America—were one of the few natural sources of a sugar hit, an intoxicating reward that repaid the toil that went into the digging. The sensual pleasure alone was an excuse to seek out the animals, but they also provided nutritional value. Glucose, fructose, and proteins in the honeypot fluid—made in the ant's body from plant nectar—quickly replenished the energy the digger expended on the search.

Known to insect specialists as repletes, these creatures are the storeholds of the colony's fortunes should normal food supplies dwindle to dangerous levels. Within the ant colony, the task is delegated to the biggest and strongest of a colony's newly emerged adults. So assigned, they retire to the lowest chambers of the nest and hang in small groups from the walls and ceiling. The fill-'er-up process begins right away, while their exoskeletons are still supple. Fed a steady dose of nectar by frenetically active sisters, the repletes' abdomens swell until the walls are stretched into a microthin, transparent membrane, the nectar gleaming like a gem within. On a dig in Colorado, Randy Morgan, curator of entomology of the Cincinnati Zoo's Insectarium, describes his first glimpse into the honeypot chamber: "In the interplay of our flashlights the repletes sparkled and glistened like living jewels. The spectacle was enough to make anybody pause spellbound."

Eventually the abdomen becomes so engorged the ant cannot move. She exists in a dreamlike expectation of utility, which comes when the colony's stores diminish and hunger sets in. Responding to the stroke of a worker's leg upon her abdomen, the replete regurgitates a drop of nectar from her mouth parts, which the worker can consume herself or re-regurgitate to another member of the colony. Aboriginal honeypot hunters claim that if mulga nectar is scarce for two years (due to drought or disease), the repletes shrink indistinguishably into the company of their worker sisters.

In better times, the repletes' abdomens can grow to the size of small grapes. Morgan describes his technique for tasting the nectar: "The head and thorax are held snugly between thumb and forefinger, so they don't have any wiggle room." Mandible nips are not an issue, he says, because "they are weak biters, and fingertip skin is tough." Placing the abdomen between his lips, he "tightly pinched their bodies as I popped the abdomen; this way they are euthanized quickly and painlessly." The initial taste is of bitter/sour formic acid, followed by a quick gush of sweetness. Morgan likens it to cane molasses. In some Mexican markets, the ants are sold according to the color and flavor of the nectar: from deep brown (called "Coca-Cola ants") to dark yellow ("butter") to pale ("vinegar").

In Australia, the animal has been important to indigenous peoples not only as a food source, but as a spiritual totem. Aboriginal creation myth holds that during dreamtime, men and women descended from a panoply of animals, plants, and things, each with its own specific pathways across the countryside, its own songs, dances, and rituals. The honeypot ant (known variously as *yerumpa*, *tjala*, and *woma* in Aboriginal languages) is an important clan emblem within this intricate system.

Today it's less common than in times past for people to dig for honeypots, the main exceptions being schoolchildren learning about traditional foraging and tour groups seeking authentic Australian bush tucker. The honeypot ant has, meanwhile, found an alternate career as a model. From its starting point as the subject of Aboriginal dreamtime paintings, it has moved on to colonize postcards, T-shirts, and coffee cups. Underground, oblivious, a replete lives in her own dreamtime, waiting to release her riches.

Honeysuckle

It's a stretch to call honeysuckle a food, but the tiny drop of nectar the flower yields to a patient-fingered child is, once tasted, an indelible flavor of summer. The nectar is sweet and free, and so are July afternoons, standing within a cascade of the vines' heady flowers until dinner is ready and it's time to go home.

In his poem "To Earthward," Robert Frost evokes the taste memory:

> *I had the swirl and ache*
> *From sprays of honeysuckle*
> *That when they're gathered shake*
> *Dew on the knuckle*
>
> *I craved strong sweets, but those*
> *Seemed strong when I was young . . .*

A writer in 1916, unknown, is more explicit on the flower's allure:

When daylight begins to fade, these long, slender-tubed buds ex-pand to welcome their chosen benefactors, the sphinx moths, woo-ing them with fragrance so especially strong and sweet at this time that, long after dark, guests may be guided from afar by it alone, and entertaining them with copious draughts of deeply hidden nectar, which their long tongues alone may drain. . . . Rough, rounded pollen grains, carried on the hairs and scales on the under side of the moth's body from his head to his abdomen, including antennae, tongue, legs, and wings, cannot but be rubbed off on the protruding sticky stigma of the next honeysuckle tube entered.

For all its slender, trembling grace, the plant has a will of steel. Southerners are incredulous that northern nurseries sell it as a decorative creeper, for in warmer climes the plant escalates from creeping to strangling. The St. Louis County Parks Department holds honeysuckle-eradication weekends to clear the plant from Missouri forests' understory, to prevent the plant from muscling out other species by blocking the sunlight. Dan Huntley, writing in the *Charlotte Observer* in 2000, made clear his exasperation at the vine that was taking over his garden: "If azaleas and magnolias are the country club elites of the plant world, honeysuckle is the low-rent trash."

The lesson: leave honeysuckle to a neighboring homeowner, soon enough it'll be as good as yours. To sample the nectar, pluck a white flower from the vine. Pinch the star-shaped green calyx at the base and slowly draw the stamen assembly back through the long throat. A translucent bead of nectar will gather at the tip of a stalk, which you touch to your tongue. If the flower is especially full, a drop or two can be sipped from the now-hollow bloom, as if it's a straw.

Few experiences of such fleeting sweetness as sipping honeysuckle leave as deep-seated memories as this; one other is teaching your own child how to do it.

Human Placenta

Even the most gung-ho extreme-food promoters on the planet—the producers of the TV show *Survivor*—didn't dare present one tidbit that is eaten sporadically but steadily in the United States and abroad. If offered a plate of human placenta, the contestants would revolt, the viewing audience would revolt, and the organ, which has experienced one rejection after another since birth, would be unanimously voted off the island, in a bright yellow medical waste bag.

Placenta is one of those foods, like black-eyed peas, whose appeal is largely a matter of time and place. In this case, the time/place locus is after a home birth, when the hormones of unanesthetized mothers are rocketing off the charts and male partners are so pumped by the blessed miracle they're willing to try anything just to keep up. There are no figures available on how many people sample placenta. It is safe to say that they are an elite cadre within the already selective home-birthing corps.

And they'd have to be. Just look at the thing. No, go on, look at it. A thickly veined maroon clump of tissue approximately the size and thickness of an inflated whoopee cushion, possibly lumpy with the calcification that sets in at the end of pregnancy, with a fluorescent blue, tightly coiled umbilical cord attached to one side. It's not exactly filet mignon visually speaking, but all respect is nonetheless due. It was the anatomical interface between symbiont and host: nutrient/waste processor, oxygen/CO_2 regulator and systemic firewall, allowing two different genetic codes to coexist in one body.

In the kingdom of mammals, everybody loves placenta except humans, certain seals, and whales. Even animals that are otherwise vegetarian relish it. It is no easy matter for creatures whose teeth and jaws are adapted for tender fruit and veggies to get a placenta and the associated fetal membranes down; in some ways it is labor twice over. Finishing may take an hour or more, while the newborn patiently waits for some attention.

Why do animals devour placenta? Are they so ravenous from giving birth that they'll eat anything nearby? Does the organ contain nutrients that the new mother craves? Is she trying to keep the birth area clean to deter predators? The question haunted Mark B. Kristal of the Department of Psychology at the University at Buffalo. He brought the full powers of his laboratory to bear in finding the answer, and in 1980 he published the results in *Neuroscience and Biobehavioral Reviews*.

Over many trials, the rodents he observed were kept virginal, made pregnant, allowed to give birth naturally, C-sectioned, hysterectomized, injected with hormones, given brain lesions, and, through it all, presented dish after dish of placenta. The upshot? The scientists were able to discount the eat-anything-nearby theory, as rats won't touch any other meat provided. Likewise the keeping-the-nest-clean theory, since arboreal monkeys can simply drop the placenta out of the tree after giving birth, but would rather eat it. The team did learn some fascinating things, including:

- Most virgin rodents are freaked when presented with placenta, to the point where they turn tail and quiver, or try to leap away from the dish in their cage.

- If given the choice between all-you-can-eat placenta and chocolate-chip cookies, new-mother rodents refuse the cookies and eat as many as forty to sixty placentas in four hours' time.

- Right after delivery, it is easier to take a pup away from a mother rat than it is to take the placenta.

Kristal cites another researcher, H. G. Birch, who ventured that the reason so many mammals lick their newborns clean is not because they love the babies, it's because they love the way the babies taste: like placenta.

In 1991, Professor Kristal published a follow-up review of further research. In this one, also for *Neuroscience and Biobehavioral Reviews*, is an astonishing revelation. In rodents, a component of placenta and amniotic fluid called placenta opioid-enhancing factor (POEF for short) markedly boosts the painkilling effects of the body's natural opioids, which flood the maternal system during the stresses of birth. Consuming afterbirth—and only consuming it; injections of it don't work—eases the mother's pain and presumably chills her out, allowing her to get down to the business of caring for her young. The effects can be measured within five minutes after the mother begins licking leaked amniotic fluid from her vulva, and last about thirty to forty minutes after the placenta is eaten.

This same component is also present in human placenta and amniotic fluid. For reasons not entirely clear, our species is not in the habit of taking advantage of this homegrown POEF, but one cannot help but wonder how the experience of childbirth might be different if we did.

In fact, placenta-eating among humans has been reported so infrequently in non-Western populations as to barely register on the anthropological database. Most cultures are content to give the placenta a burial with honors, say a few chants, and move on. Only in contemporary America and England do people devise recipes for placenta pizza (cooking instructions are available on the web, along with many other dishes to tempt the new baby's admirers).

If the eat-your-placenta movement gains ground in the United States, it will be largely due to the encouragement of those midwives who believe doing so bestows considerable benefits. Their list includes offsetting maternal hemorrhage, greater overall strength, and reduced likelihood of postnatal depression. None of these effects have been verified in an orthodox scientific study, but neither have they been tested in one. Placenta may be beneficial in another way as well: in an unrigorous experiment conducted in Czechoslovakia in the 1950s, cited by Kristal, eating freeze-dried placenta improved milk flow.

If circumstances find you, a placenta, and a cutting board in the same general vicinity, here are some rough guidelines for its preparation. Opinion differs on whether the organ should be eaten raw or cooked. You, as a disinterested third party, are probably aware that any POEF molecules will likely be destroyed by cooking, but best to stay out of this argument and let the mother and midwife hash it out. If raw wins, saw (the outer membranes are tough) a small chunk off the maternal side of the organ (the one opposite the birth cord). Give it to the mother to tuck between cheek and gum. If cooked placenta is desired, cut away the exterior membranes. Then stew, stir-fry, dehydrate, powder, grind into a pâté, or a puree into a Bloody Mary (again, the internet has recipes by the score). Even committed vegetarians can be convinced to try placenta, since no animal was killed in its name, and indeed it is the ultimate life-giver.

The other red meat: is there any harm in eating it? Some argue that, if taken raw, it could transmit AIDS, hepatitis, or other infectious diseases, if the mother herself is a carrier. Also, since eating it is a kind of cannibalism, the question arises as to whether it might be a pathway for the brain-wasting diseases that occur when humans or animals eat their own kind. Again, since no orthodox studies have been done, there is no way of saying definitively.

The cannibalism issue is one of the standard objections to placenta pizza (one that an extra-cheese option will not overcome). But if eating this by-product of pregnancy is venturing into the ultimate taboo, then isn't that also true of chewing a fingernail or kissing away the tears of a child, not to mention all the other bodily fluids—at least one containing live gametes—that humans go in for? If we swallow—lustily—the precursors to childbirth, is it really so strange to have a bite or two of the aftermath?

Jellyfish

A walk along the coastal beaches of South Carolina, Georgia, and Florida at dawn in late spring holds a fascinating sight: up and down the wave wash, gleaming in the rising sun, are fist-sized, stingerless rubbery orbs with a rippling frill at the base: *Stomolophus meleagris*, better known locally as jellyballs or cannonball jellyfish. The big gray-and-white gulls that patrol these shores take a few heartless pecks at the dying blobs, then move on to more flavorful prey. It is a reminder of the harsh order of nature, but we shouldn't feel too sorry for the jellyfish. They're heartless too, as well as boneless, liverless, and brainless. As far as sentience goes, they're only slightly brighter than Jell-O.

Slackers that they are, they're also marvelous creatures—an example of what nature can whip up with a few basic ingredients. Some collagen to give the bell its shape, a mucous polysaccharide filler, some minerals, and a whole lot of water, the latter adding up to 95 percent of the animal's total bulk. Jellyballs are a more burly and thick-skinned species than their gossamer, stinger-trailing brethren. They can manage without tentacles thanks to the thick layer of mucus on the oral frill, which captures larval shellfish and plankton and draws them in toward its mouth.

A decade ago, the shrimpers and other fishermen working the waters considered the animals pests, for they fouled the nets and occupied space better taken up by profitable creatures, like shrimp and fish. Recently, though, there's been a small-scale turnaround. A few of the same fishermen who badmouthed the jellies as junk have been selling them to wholesalers in the Far East, who in turn are feeding that region's massive appetite for the creature.

Gulls may disdain them, but jellyfish are a delicacy, especially in China, where they have been eaten for at least 1,700 years. The creatures are imported by the ton from other countries thanks to their thick skin, which gives the chewy crunch so appreciated by connoisseurs. This aspect of Chinese gastronomy, the *kou gan* or mouthfeel of a dish, is considered a sensual experience on par with the flavor and appearance. Kou gan goes a long way toward explaining why so many consumables ignored by other cultures (squishy, slimy, scaly, too many legs) have found a place on the Chinese menu.

A brief aside: Americans, especially American kids, are also crazy for mouthfeel, but only if the overriding flavor is sweet. In the candy aisle, makers offer an ever-expanding range of textural stimuli: goopy, sticky, squirty, gummy, powdery, waxy, even slimy. As long as it's sugary, anything goes. Take that away and all bets are off. We'll happily eat gummy worms, but shudder at aspic (which shudders back).

And this, the texture, is what eating jellyfish is all about, because any animal comprised largely of water is not going to offer much in the flavor department. In fact, if a jellyfish tastes like anything, it's the salt water in which it has been processed, a monthlong procedure in which the animal is dried, shredded, and packaged, to be reconstituted by the cook for the table in a bath of boiling water. A typical preparation is a salad made of jellyfish strips, shredded carrot, and spring onions, dressed in a light soy and vinegar sauce. When all is said and done, the experience is kind of *eh*, much like eating those thick translucent rice noodles that are found in Asian soups and salads.

Still, those who hold jellyfish in high regard are on to something, and not only on the texture-appreciation front. In 2005 Professor Yun-Hwa Peggy Hsieh was issued a U.S. patent covering the extraction and formulation of jellyfish collagen as a treatment for rheumatoid arthritis. This boneless creature, living the gelatinous lifestyle in the waves, may ultimately show stiff human joints how to hang loose and relax.

Jerusalem Artichoke

Here's a tip if you want to cook dinner as part of a romantic date. Do not, under any circumstances, prepare a dish made with Jerusalem artichokes, especially if it's date number three. For later the same evening, you and your paramour will experience flatulence so explosive in force, so cubic in volume, and so fetid in smell that romance will fly right out the window—the window you must fling open to get life-sustaining fresh air. There is no point trying to suppress flatulence like this. You will blow up. Save Jerusalem artichoke for dinner when your mother-in-law comes over, once your true love is bound by vows to stay with you.

In more rustic times, when rude noises around the campfire were par for the course, Jerusalem artichokes were a savior for people seeking forage in hardscrabble territory. On their expedition westward, Lewis and Clark turned to their native guide Sacagawea, who knew just where to look:

When we halted for dinner she [Sacagawea] busied herself in searching for the wild artichokes which the mice collect and deposit in large hoards. This operation she performed by penetrating the earth with a sharp stick about some small collection of driftwood. Her labour soon proved successful and she procured a good quantity of these roots. (Captain Meriwether Lewis, April 9, 1805)

While it might seem surprising that a tuber called Jerusalem artichoke could be readily found on American frontier soil, this is in fact a native American vegetable in all senses. French explorer Samuel de Champlain was the first European to describe it. In 1605, he came across it growing in Cape Cod gardens that were tilled by the native Eastern Abenaki people. He took some of the easy-to-grow tubers back with him to France. With time they grew popular enough to be sold by Parisian street vendors, who called them *topinambours,* after a completely unrelated tribe another explorer had found in Brazil. The vegetable seems to inspire creative naming. It continued in Italy, where its Italian name, *girasole articiocco,* translates as "sunflower artichoke." This is basically accurate because the plant is a member of the sunflower family, and the cooked tuber tastes a bit like artichoke. But somewhere down the line, the Italian name got corrupted into "Jerusalem," a place where it never existed and where it would never grow, as it appreciates a snappy winter frost. The tradition continues today, with some American vendors calling them "sunchokes." This may be a ploy to distract from the vegetables' unprepossessing appearance. They are indeed soil-ridden, gnarled thick fingers of a tuber. At one low point in the past their looks put off continental diners, who believed, on the principle that you are what you eat, that sunchokes would give you leprosy.

But enough about their looks; more about their notorious effect on the digestive system. Here, some organic chemistry comes into play. The tubers contain a starchlike carbohydrate known as inulin, which in chemical terms is an oligosaccharide. Simply stated, an oligosaccharide is made up of energy packets (in this case fructose and glucose) linked together in a chain. Another vegetable that contains oligosaccharides is, not coincidentally, beans. The Jerusalem artichoke stores inulin in its rootlike tubers to power new growth come spring. Unless a harvester unearths it in late fall, in which case the tuber is scrubbed, then steamed, boiled, baked, stir-fried, or eaten raw as a crudité. Which is fitting terminology for what happens next.

Inulin, unlike the starch found in potatoes, can't be digested by the stomach and small intestine; our enzymes aren't made to crack it. So the molecules pass through the system intact until they come to the colon. Here they meet the local bacteria, and the two, in effect, go to war. It's Armageddon in there until the inulin is finally broken up, which happens with a spectacular scorched-earth release of carbon dioxide and methane gas. Or scorched sheets, sofa, what have you. The point is, it's got to go somewhere, and that somewhere is out.

Jerusalem artichoke experts say that the effect can be lessened by keeping the tubers in the ground for a month after the first frost (if you grow them yourself) or keeping them in the fridge for a while (if you buy them). This is also said to boost their sweet taste. It's probably worth a try, but it's probably also gracious to warn innocent diners that turbulence is forecast under their covers. We can be but grateful that due to some accident of history, this Native American gift to the colonizers never made the must-cook list for the Thanksgiving table. The post-dinner bowl games would go into overtime, and you know we're not talking about football.

Lichen

Of the multitude of life-forms existing on earth, the humble lichen may be the ultimate survivor. They've got the numbers, forming an entire division of fungi, with eight orders, forty-five families, and six thousand species to their credit. Lichens' hardiest cadre can withstand Antarctic winters by shutting down photosynthesis and existing in suspended animation until temperatures climb back to zero. Other species make their homes in jungles or deserts, and many thrive where the only apparent source of nutrients is the boulders on which they grow. Lichens can literally eat rock—as well as dead trees, cement, and the shells of especially slow-moving tortoises.

Most people don't pay lichens much attention, dismissing them as nature's version of shag carpet, eking out a living at so unhurried a pace that grass growth is breakneck in comparison. Botanists know otherwise. When they look at a lichen, they see an odd couple that's living together and making it work. One whose teamwork allows both partners to surpass their individual limitations and take on the world as an all-powerful unit.

The next lichen you see, no matter where or when, is not one being but two—an alga and a fungus bound in a symbiotic relationship. The fungus gives the team its shape (alga on its own is slip-slidey pond scum). It also provides the tethering tendrils and stone-cutting acids that allow lichen to bed into rock, drawing moisture and nutrients. The alga, for its part, contributes a photosynthesis factory that provides far more energy than the fungus could manage on its own. All in all, it's win-win, but there's a darker side to the story. Some botanists theorize that the algal element is a *captive* of the fungus. So while the relationship may be sicker below than it seems on the surface, whose isn't? It's still one hell of an organism.

And it's one whose own survival skills have saved the lives of many a snowbound explorer—most notably those in the team of John Franklin of England, who voyaged across northern Canada in 1819–22. John Back, a midshipman in the party, describes one particularly bleak evening in camp: "We scarcely got more than four miles before we halted for the night and made a meal of *tripe de roche* [rock tripe, an edible lichen] and shoe leather."

It was probably a toss-up as to which tasted better. Rock tripe, a member of the *Umbilicaria* genus, grows in large dark patches, attached to rock by a central strand. In winter it is tough and leathery in the thicker portions of its thallus, or body, but paper-thin and crumbling toward the edges. When wet, it absorbs water and develops a slimy coat. It routinely shows up in manuals like the *U.S. Army Survival Handbook* as an edible plant. Scientists at the toxicology division of Sweden's National Food Administration tested it on mice as a survival food. They found that rodents fed the lichen as a supplement not only did as well as their nonpartaking cagemates, but their immune-cell function was boosted some 40 percent.

In North America, rock tripe has traditionally been eaten as a survival food, scraped off an exposed boulder in the dead of winter and, optimally, boiled to remove some of its bitterness. At most, it fended off starvation. Compare this situation to that in Japan, where this same item is eaten as a fancy food. Here it is called *iwatake*, and it is served in a wide number of presentations, including tempura, soup, or rolled as a wrapper for sushi. According to Japanese food expert Richard Hosking, in his 1994 paper "Some Japanese Food Rarities" for the Oxford Symposium on Food and Cookery:

The most interesting thing about iwatake is the manner of harvesting, which is one by abseiling (rappelling). The harvester climbs to the top of the cliff and abseils down the face until he encounters some of the lichen, which he collects by scraping it off with a knife. There are very few people now who are prepared to do this, and they are quite old. There is a real danger that when they are gone, the iwatake will remain on their cliff-faces, mostly in the island of Shikoku, indefinitely.

There is one significant commonality between Japanese and North American rock tripe consumption, as Hosking reveals: "Why they are harvested at all is something of a mystery, considering the dangers involved and the fact that no-one enjoys the 'flavour' of them anyway . . . the thing people most enjoy about them is to be eating something a hundred or more years old, as if the eaters were hoping to gain the longevity of the 'mushrooms' through eating them."

Longevity. The same thing explorer Franklin and his companions were hoping for—and found, thanks to eating this most unlikely delicacy.

Live Monkey Brain

No book with the title *Fierce Food* would be complete without an entry on monkey brains. It is, overwhelmingly, first and foremost on the list of the most disgusting, depraved, and wretched foods man is reported to swallow.

A quick fill-in for those few readers who may be unfamiliar with this phenomenon. Allegedly, in places in the Far East—typically somewhere in China—banquets take place where the pièce de résistance is the living brain of a monkey. The monkey has been strapped into a special table that has a monkey-head-sized hole drilled through it. With the top of its head exposed, the animal is shaved (sometimes), bludgeoned unconscious (sometimes), then its skull is sawn through (always). Diners scoop out the still-pulsing brain, adding condiments of their choice. Monkey-brain banquets were presented in two notorious shockumentaries, *Mondo Cane* (1962) and *Faces of Death* (1978), and fictionally in *Indiana Jones and the Temple of Doom*.

So there, in all its horror, is the live-monkey-brain gorefest. It takes the imagination hostage in a really unpleasant way, especially if it's late at night and you're all alone in the house.

But there's another aspect to the story that is not entirely unwelcome. Though few people are likely to admit it, at the same time that the practice repulses, it also gives a low thrill. Deep down, we reckon that people who are doing something so very bad to helpless screaming creatures are in for some massive karmic payback. AIDS, SARS, the mother of all typhoons: retribution's coming, and whatever it is, it's going to be good.

But here's the thing. As fierce foods go, this one is bullshit. In fact, it's safe to say that more people on earth routinely eat bullshit (see "Dung Beetle Larvae," "Pia") than eat live monkey brains. The film footage in the three movies mentioned earlier is roundly derided by FX-savvy fourteen-year-olds. The tables with holes in them that are offered up as evidence were actually made to hold hot pots on the boil. Reporters based in the Far East who have made in-depth investigations of the subject are conclusive in their debunking. One of them is Paul Levy, a highly respected food journalist and author who has traveled and eaten widely in Asia. He traces the roots of the story to a hoax enacted by Singapore journalists to trick one of their comrades into printing something outlandish. Levy further claims that his many formidable Hong Kong food connections have never personally witnessed any such meal taking place. It is, he thunders, in print, and later, when asked in person, "at bottom a canard." *Canard* can mean either a duck or a groundless rumor. He doesn't mean duck.

D. Eric Franks of Maxent.org, and mastermind behind the web's number-one page on eating monkey brains, agrees. In a long and carefully sourced article, he concludes that "eating live monkey brains as a delicacy is highly unlikely and the canonical tales are almost certainly not true." In personal correspondence, he drills it down: "I am arguing that the legend that 'Chinese people eat [live] monkey brains' is false."

So it's not a habitual act. It's probably not even an occasional act. (Today it is illegal in China to serve or eat wildlife, and with the onset of the disease SARS, the authorities are increasingly aggressive in their enforcement). But could it have happened somewhere, ever? Of course. Possibly in centuries past, as is claimed in the mid-nineteenth-century travelogue by Zhang Hai Ou called *Casual Chat on Man Tuo Lou's Veranda*. Possibly in recent times, in the environs of the Pingxiang game market near China's border with Vietnam, where, according to a 1998 Hong Kong tabloid article cited by Franks, such dinners were routine. Or possibly in the 1940s in Singapore, where a meal of live monkey brains was not unheard of for ethnic Chinese, as Cecil Adams related in a *Straight Dope* article in 2001.

The problem with any report of live monkey brain consumption, including this entry, is that it gives an idea wider play than it might have had otherwise. Ghouls with deep pockets might be inclined to fabricate a "delicacy" that unscrupulous traders would be pleased to help stage. A market created for live monkey brains—not by the local people, but by visitors. Visitors who, like the sex-tour pedophiles traveling to Southeast Asia, are happy to keep the business, and the shame, in somebody else's backyard.

Locust

What's the difference between a grasshopper and a locust? Grasshoppers are stay-at-home types, minding their own business down in the meadow, getting together with other grasshoppers only when nature says it's time to get

busy. Locusts, in contrast, are party animals. They love a road trip like frat brothers on spring break, traveling up to eighty
miles in a single day in swarms that could
easily blanket Daytona.

Since the dawn of agriculture,
these finger-length creatures have
inspired fear and loathing for the devastation they bring, blotting the sky in a glitter-
ing cloud that moves faster than the wind,
descending in a rasping whir of
wings as loud as a hailstorm to
devour every piece of vegetation in
sight. Proposed locust-control methods
have kept stride with technology, ranging from giant nets and enormous vac-
uum cleaners to flamethrowers and
lasers. None of these work to any
reasonable degree. Pesticides, with
all the attendant environmental
hazards, are still the most effective means
to keep them in check. But humans can get their own
back in another way, taking them out one at a time.

During his time in the wilderness, John the Baptist
liked to eat them with wild honey. Cambodians stuff the
gut with a peanut, then wok-fry them. Table-ready locusts
and grasshoppers are found in market stalls around the
world, a cheap source of protein with percentages compa-
rable to beef. As a bonus, nearly everyone who tries them
is pleasantly surprised by how good they taste. Depending on the preparation, the flavor has been compared to

cooked egg yolk, fried fish stuffed with buttered toast, or smoky bacon.

Unless you're a survivalist, it's unlikely you'll ever need to prepare your own locust from scratch, but it never hurts to know how it's done.

The first step is boiling the live bug for ten minutes. This accomplishes four things. First, it helps clean off pesticide (beware: if the animal has been exposed, some will stay in its system no matter how carefully you wash). Second, it renders the hard exoskeleton more pliable for the next stage of preparation. Third, it neutralizes nematodes and other parasites living in the creature's gut (yes, you might get a two-for-one deal with a locust). Finally, and most important, it kills the animal, simplifying the next step, which is plucking off the wings, forelegs, and the spindly end section of the hind legs. These tend to get stuck in the teeth and compound any constipation you may suffer from eating the animal's indigestible outer casing. The head should also be gently twisted off, slowly dragging out any guts that may be attached.

Thus dressed, the locust is ready for frying, roasting, or barbecuing on a stick. If you're still hesitant, it may help to remember that French-speaking Africans are only half-joking when they call locusts *crevettes du Sahara*, or desert shrimp.

Maguey Worm

Restaurante Bar "Chon" on Regina Street in Mexico City is a temple of fierce food. A pre-Columbian temple, where acolytes willingly sacrifice their wallets to appease their cravings for the creepy, the crawly, and the deservedly obscure: crocodile, ant eggs, grasshoppers, and much, much more.

Looking around, you'd never guess this was the foremost purveyor of pre-Hispanic cuisine in the world. You walk in, wait by the stuffed armadillo at the entrance to be seated, and take your place at one of the twenty or so four-tops. It looks like so many other airy, comfortable lunchrooms that welcome hearty eaters of all kinds, from local workers (with healthy pocketbooks — Don Chon is not shy when it comes to pricing) to politicians cutting deals to visiting notables who want a taste of Mexico at its most exotic. Over in the corner, a TV plays boxing matches, and a clutch of white-aproned waiters gathers by the bar to watch if business is slow. In the kitchen, two women are visible just past the door chopping, boning, and working the stove.

You've ordered an appetizer of deep-fried maguey worm, known locally as *gusanos*. This animal is familiar to most of us as that li'l critter at the bottom of the mezcal bottle that — wait, now there's two. *Whoa.* OK, back to one, but it's starting to spin . . .

It's a little-known fact that the worm was not put in the bottle as a test of machismo for hard-drinking collegiates. Nor is it hallucinogenic, or aphrodisiac, as is often claimed. *Eat the Worm* is a marketing line rather than an intrinsic part of mezcal lore. The larva is there to demonstrate the purity and high proof of the alcohol content rather than the utter pollutedness of the drinker.

The worm is harvested from the maguey cactus, a desert plant with thick gray-green leaves. Riddling these leaves in June and October are the caterpillars of the *Aegiale hesperialis* butterfly, which harvesters extract with a hook, grabbing the worms' heads and carefully drawing them out. *Mescaleros* in the countryside sell them to distributors in larger towns, who in turn send them to restaurants like Restaurante Bar "Chon."

The bigger of the worms are as long as a pinkie; deep-fried, their once-pale segmented bodies are now bolt-straight, slightly flattened, and golden brown. A glistening heap comes with a side of some of the best guacamole you'll ever taste. And the worms themselves are startlingly good. Crunchy-light and savory, they are a fine snack food for watching the fights, tasting much like those few very brown, very crisp, overcooked french fries that always get trapped in the bottom of the fast-food bag. If they didn't look so much like worms these things would find a much larger fan base up north.

As it stands, most Americans who have tried gusanos have done so at the bottom of the bottle, and their memories of it are hazy at best. Trust us: It's possible to like the fried ones in a completely sober state. Just head south and turn right at the stuffed armadillo.

Manna

The Lord said to Moses, "I am going to rain bread from heaven for you, and each day the people shall go out and gather enough for that day"... When the layer of dew lifted, there on the surface of the wilderness was a fine flaky substance, as fine as frost on the ground. When the Israelites saw it, they said to one another, "What is it?" for they did not know what it was. Moses said to them, "It is the bread that the Lord has given you to eat."... The house of Israel called it manna; it was like coriander seed, white, and the taste of it was like wafers made with honey. (Exodus 16: 4–31)

In the night it shall fall in small drops on the reeds, which they shall gather and beat with clubs, and then will it taste very sweet, and having but little they will prize it the more. (Native American myth, recorded by John Wesley Powell, 1881, and recounted in *The Human Use of Insects as a Food Resource*, Gene DeFoliart, ed.)

Two different hemispheres, two different belief systems, tribes of Israelites and Californian Native Americans nourished alike by a sweet substance that seemed to rain down from the heavens. God or godlike beings take credit in both cases, but the true source of manna is tiny insects—frequently aphids—that in modern gardening circles are considered a scourge.

The Bible calls it a kind of bread, but manna is actually a flaky, crystalline material that coats grasses, reeds, leaves, and the slender branches of plants. It is most easily found in early morning. Also known as honeydew, this mysterious substance is seasonal, appearing only for a few months in the late spring and early summer. Its true identity is sap, once removed. The sap was sucked from tender leaves and twiglets by hungry aphid larvae and immature females, then digested and excreted to coat the feeding grounds. While this heavenly food may have lavatorial origins, it's about as refined as excrement gets, composed almost exclusively of sugary carbohydrates. The bugs gorge on sap, says Frederick Bodenheimer, a biologist specializing in insects of biblical lands, in order to take in its minute quantities of nitrogen, which the bugs need to keep their metabolism functioning properly. The excess is excreted in huge amounts: manna harvesters can collect a couple pounds per day.

Manna is consistently described as delicious. Frederick Vernon Colville, an anthropologist writing in 1892, tells of the preparation process by the Mojave Desert Panamint people: "When perfectly brittle the whole plant is ground and the finer portion separated by sifting. This moist, sticky flour is moulded by the hands into a thick gum-like mass. It is then set near a fire and roasted until it swells and browns slightly, and in this taffy-like state it is eaten."

In present-day Iran and Iraq, manna is harvested, strained, and mixed with eggs and nuts, then dried and sold as a sweet called *man* or *minnal simma* or *gaz*. The sticky palm-sized balls are coated in a light dusting of flour to facilitate handling. Says Ghida Damirji, whose uncle often brought the treat to her family in the United States from Iraq, the sweets occasionally lifted the brows of the customs officers at Kennedy Airport, but a sample taste of the delicious, nougaty treat quickly put paid to questions about their composition.

It may be possible to find manna close to home—as close as your car, if it's parked under an aphid-infested maple or alder tree in early summer. That sticky goo you've been scraping off the windshield, cursing at? It's honeydew, probably contaminated by pesticides or pollution. It should be cleaned off fairly quickly, or else it will develop a sooty black mold. If this seems bothersome, it may help to remember that if you'd been born in another time and place, manna harvest would be an all-day chore.

Muttonbird

The muttonbird, an oceangoing resident of Australia, New Zealand, and other islands in the South Pacific, has some identity issues. These may explain why the bird is so little known as a food outside its geographic region.

First there's the name. Early European settlers to these parts, hungry and disoriented from the long sea voyage, thought the bird tasted like sheep, and so named it muttonbird. Scientists, for their part, recognize it as the sooty shearwater. New Zealand's native Maori people, who knew it long before anyone else, call it *titi*.

In fact, muttonbird tastes like fish, which brings us to identity issue number two. It tastes so much like fish — very strong fish — that it is usually sold by fishmongers. Those in the know claim that the intensity of the marine flavor can be brought down to a palatable level by first soaking the cleaned and gutted carcass for two days (changing the water every eight hours), then boiling the bird for three hours (changing the water on an intensified hourly basis). After this pretreatment, it is ready to roast, in an oven, for an hour or so.

This technique will effectively remove some fishiness from the bird, but, in keeping with Newton's Third Law, it will equally and oppositely redistribute the oily molecules into the kitchen, household, and beyond. Preparing and cooking the bird outdoors is more sensible, as long as there is a stiff breeze and you are upwind. Even so, don't count on wearing the same clothing if company's coming and you plan on sitting anywhere near them.

Issue number three in the identity department is the muttonbird's nesting habits. Here it acts less like a bird or a sheep or a fish than a gopher, digging itself a burrow that it revisits on an annual basis. Once it has logged a thirty-thousand-kilometer round-trip of migratory air miles, it comes home to tunnel in and lay its sole egg deep in the peaty hole. This takes place in November. The hatchling appears sometime in the third week of January. It is cared for by both parents, who feed it a diet of nearly pure regurgitated fish oil. The baby gets fatter and fatter, until it eventually grows to twice the weight of either parent.

When the chick's downy nest feathers begin to give way to flight feathers in April, the adult birds say *hasta la vista*, baby, and take off, leaving the colony of young birds to party in an unsupervised environment. Most eventually fly off on migrations of their own, but about a quarter of the fledglings will fall prey to stalkers on four feet and two.

On New Zealand, muttonbirds may only be harvested by hereditary right, by people of Maori descent, during a limited season that runs from April through May. Muttonbirding is a traditional occupation that requires hardiness, craftiness, and patient tolerance for all the scientists jostling for position around the nesting sites, trying to get a bead on whether the bird populations are healthy or in decline.

The muttonbirders go about their work much as they always have, clambering over the slippery, steep fern-covered slopes, poking around in thick root systems, hanging precariously over cliffsides, in hopes of detecting a promising entrance, which may not be evident to the untrained eye. Every muttonbird colony has patches of especially ripe picking, much like an orchard features areas of particularly productive trees. Good muttonbirders know where they are. Once a burrow is located and the muttonbirder determines that a chick rests within (by using an arm or a wire to poke around), he'll dive fingers first, shoulder deep into the burrow (which can extend several yards underground) and wrestle the two-pound chick out. The bird's neck is quickly snapped. The birder next squeezes the contents of its stomach out in front of the entry, which shows to fellow hunters that the nest has been cleared.

This is the daylight, or *nanao* segment of the hunting season, which is much harder work than the *rama* period, which takes place later on, when the chicks start taking little walks outside the burrow at night. Leaving the harvest to these easier, later days would not be profitable for the muttonbirders, so they continue their daylit, waist-deep plunges into the boggy soil, hoping to snare a downy prize.

Scientists studying muttonbirds in the field work closely with the hunters, since they have the shared aim of preserving healthy stocks. Lacking the muttonbirders' generations-long mastery of the nesting colony, the scientists devised specialized equipment to monitor the situation. The burrowscope, for example. This infrared light and camera apparatus, mounted to a long hose, was intended to project an image of the tunnel's interior to a screen at the surface. While brilliant on paper, there were hiccups in practice, one problem being that it couldn't be manipulated around interior corners underground. Back to the drawing board. A second device appeared to eliminate the problem of underground blind alleys by remaining on the surface. It consisted of a modified burglar-alarm system, with a bar gate the bird triggered every time it entered and left the nest. A central control panel could monitor sixteen different burrows at a time and store records of 4,600 entries and exits. So far so good. But when the system was tested, the researchers got some very peculiar readings, indicating entries and exits of maniacal frequency, as though the chick had a jillion errands to run but kept forgetting its keys. The researchers suspect that these may have been due to "birds repeatedly tugging at the entrance bar from within the burrow, or from displacement of the bar by breathing movements of a bird sitting in the burrow's entrance."

This ecologically correct version of *Caddyshack* is sure to continue. Meanwhile, the muttonbirds' love of oily, reeking fish is still their best protection against overharvesting.

Natto

The signage is the same. The fixtures are the same. But the *natto* on the menu is definitely out of order. This is not Denny's as you know it. This is Denny's Japan-style family restaurant, a place where you can have a bowl of fermented, slime-ridden beans as a side to your breakfast-special eggs and white toast.

Whether it comes in a bowl with the Denny's logo, an artisanal pot made by a Living National Treasure, or a Styrofoam clamshell, natto is notorious among newcomers to Japan, for it is a food Japanese hosts love to serve guests as a test of their fortitude and face-control. It's the hosts' little joke, because natto is one of the smelliest and most mucosal foods ever devised by the mind of man. Even the Japanese say it takes four tries before you really begin to appreciate its special savor. Some people do like it right from the start—these tend to be the kind of people who voluntarily eat liverwurst, or carry stinky cheese on public transport during rush hour.

At the Tokyo Denny's, the bowl contains half a cup of small brown beans that are covered with a scattering of chopped scallions, a dab of strong mustard, and a white film that looks alarmingly like mildew. An exploratory stir and lift with the chopsticks reveals that the beans are held together by sticky strands. The strands are remarkably stretchy, capable of extending waaaaaay far—as far as three feet from chopsticks held at altitude to base camp in the bowl. The experiment leaves microfine filaments trailing hither and thither all over the table, from teapot to soy sauce bottle to menu stand. All in all, the slime is remarkably similar to the kind the aliens lay down when they're marking their territory on the spaceship.

People have eaten natto in Japan for centuries. It was created, as these things tend to be, by accident. The sliminess of the beans results from fermentation by the bacterium *Bacillus natto*, a microbe that occurs naturally in rice straw. Food historians theorize that natto came to be when a container of cooked soybeans was stored in or nearby the straw and was forgotten for a while, during which time the bacteria got in and went to work, creating the strong flavor and stringy webs. A very hungry person rediscovered the bowl, braved the contents, and against all odds liked it well enough to replicate the process on purpose. Today, natto is made in industrial quantities with special small soybeans that ferment quickly. These are steamed, sprayed with *Bacillus natto*, salt, sugar, and yeast, and then stored at 40°C for twenty-four hours. They are then aged for a week at 0°C. At this point they are table ready, and consumed to the tune of fifty thousand tons annually in Japan.

The chopsticks are poised, the slime tendrils are billowing, it's time to taste the natto. Instantly the taste buds are rammed, SWAT-style, with the lumpy sensation of beans that were marinated in ammonia then coated with a substance not dissimilar to fresh Super Glue. The taste is uncompromising, especially if the mustard isn't evenly mixed in. Microfine sticky strands tether your lips to the beans in the bowl, then break free and flutter over the napkin holder. Natto is deeply, deeply weird food. Anything that tastes as funky as this has got to be extraordinarily good for you.

Research has proven this to be so. The beans are packed with phytoestrogens, which may explain why Japanese women are three times less likely to die from breast cancer than Americans, though the link has been called into question. The beans also contain vitamin K, an important nutrient, as well as pyrazine, a substance that reduces the occurrence of blood clots.

If you find yourself living in Japan and you have duly given natto the regulation four tries, you may find that you've become a convert. At this point you can spread your wings and try the many varieties found throughout the country: *mito natto*, made from extra-small soybeans; *hikiwari natto*, made from split-roasted beans; dried salty natto, popped in the mouth as a snack; and, most tempting of all, *yukiwari natto*, which translates as "finger-lickin'" and is made from minced natto, rice *koji* (a special mold used to brew sake), and salt. With a name like that, it's got to be so tasty. Or maybe lickin' your fingers is the only way to get rid of the slime . . .

Nettle

Nature has given the stinging nettle plant a formidable perimeter defense system. The stalk, stems, and leaves bristle with two-millimeter-long, needle-sharp hairs called trichomes. They're intended to keep away grazers, but they make no distinction between an animal's muzzle and your bare skin. Brushing up against them trips the touch-sensitive bulbs, shooting a potent chemical cocktail (which includes histamine, the same agent that gives bee venom its sting) up the trichomes' hollow shafts and out through the beveled, hypodermic-needle-like tips. You have been nailed. Within seconds the affected tissue begins to swell, and small white itchy spots called wheals erupt on the skin. Within three to five minutes the itching, searing, maddening pain of a nettle sting hits its peak, and you're a truly unhappy camper, or hiker, or whatever it is you're doing out in nature in the first place. Mercifully, the torment is short-lived, and after an hour, the symptoms largely disappear, apart from an occasional tingle.

Oddly enough, people—especially in the United Kingdom and northern Europe—eat this plant, donning heavy gloves to harvest it from the shady spots it prefers at the edges of fields and wooded trails. Long ago, someone discovered that the nettle's sting is disarmed with a few minutes of cooking at high heat. This transforms it into a tender and exceedingly nutritious spring green, which is usually served boiled, steamed, or sautéed. It has a slightly bitter, deep-green taste resembling that of spinach. In Victorian England, people made a spring tonic pick-me-up by steeping the leaves like tea.

Odder still, people also eat the plant without cooking it first. The toxins may set the delicate tissues of their mouths and throats ablaze, but they are not afraid. Indeed, they are merry, for they are taking part in a contest, with a prize for whoever consumes the longest measure of raw plant. Perhaps needless to say, drinking is also involved, to the pleasure of Shane Pym, who hosts the contest at his Bottle Inn in the village of Marshwood, in the Dorset region of England. Competitive nettle eaters know a secret: the trichomes are found on the tops of the leaves, and if they are properly rolled or folded and kept away from the lips, eaters can avoid the worst of the pain. Still, the haste with which these contestants eat the nettles tends to work against precision in rolling. Shane reports that "we've never had any medical reactions, other than vomiting; it's much easier to eat nettles than it is to keep them down." He believes that Real Ale served at room temperature is the ideal liquid accompaniment, as this seems to aid in digestion. In 2005, the winner ate forty-eight stem-feet's worth. More stunning still than the sheer amount of stinging plant leaves consumed is the fact that the winner outdid forty-one other contestants, who also thought participating would be fun.

Oddest of all, some people do not stop short at eating the raw plant. In fact, nettle eaters are wimps compared to the small but stalwart group of individuals who enjoy using the fresh stalks as torture instruments in sex play. The practices of "sado-botany" are described in some detail on the internet. According to these pages, nettles are boldly going where no greens have gone before, except for the occasional cucumber and zucchini.

And so, nettle-whippers (possibly in your very neighborhood) apply the highly evolved defenses of a woodland weed to their own debauched ends. The Victorians spin like tops in their graves. And come springtime in Dorset, contestants munch their way through a chopped salad that, on behalf of plant foods the world over, unmistakably registers its offense.

Nutria

Federal, state, and local agencies came under fire for the extent of the devastation wrought by Hurricane Katrina in Louisiana in 2005. But there was another, nongovernmental agent at work undermining the bulwarks, one that has largely evaded responsibility, at least in the eyes of the public. It is an animal called the nutria—better known locally as nutra rat—a hefty rodent of foreign origin that has made a home in Gulf state wetlands. Since it came to the area at the turn of the century, it has gnawed its way through the marshes' underpinnings and riddled the levees with runways and burrows.

Since it only eats low-cal vegetation, the nutria is perpetually hungry, devouring up to 25 percent of its body weight every day. Its preferred foods are the roots and lower stems of tender marsh grasses. This is a problem because in these wetlands, the tangled and matted roots are the only thing keeping the liquid mud substrate in place. Once the nutria works its way through a given area, the tidewater breaks simply wash away. A prehurricane aerial survey of Louisiana wetlands in 2005 found that over fifty thousand acres' worth of damage was directly related to nutria feeding patterns. As bad as this sounds, state officials must have been pleased, for that was only half as bad as the acreage lost in 1998.

Just by doing what comes naturally, this nearsighted, buck-toothed, humpbacked varmint has managed to become a colossal pest. Which isn't entirely its own fault; as usual, humans share some of the blame. The animal, which originated in South America, was imported to the United States in the early part of the twentieth century as a source of trimming fur. For a number of reasons the business did not succeed and the animals were released to the wild.

The introduction of a nonnative species to a new environment is almost always a bad idea, and this case was no different. The swamp provides both an all-you-can-eat buffet and the unfettered privileges of love in the wild, which the creature exploits to the fullest. The females produce up to three litters a year, and are willing to mate the day after delivery. Gators do their part to downsize the population, but the reptiles are dormant for months at a time. The upshot: thirteen animals released in Louisiana in 1937 begot, by the late 1950s, an estimated twenty million. Nobody knows how many there are now. The nutria started out as guests with benefits. They turned into the squatters from hell.

In 1998, the state of Louisiana's Wildlife and Fisheries department, at wit's end over the nutria situation, came up with a cunning plan. Gator had found its way onto big-ticket restaurant menus. Visitors likewise suspended their qualms about okra, as long as it was in a gumbo or deep-fried. Why not promote nutra rat as a local *delicacy*, taking it out of the swamp kitchens and into restaurants with white linen tablecloths? Remarkably, a program was funded, to the tune of two million dollars. Professional chef Philippe Parola was brought in to develop recipes such as "Heart Healthy Crock-Pot Nutria" and "Ragondin with Blackberry Demi-Glace" (*ragondin* being the French name for the animal, which wouldn't fool locals, but could be the way forward with the tourists).

As campaigns go, the great nutria rehabilitation was impressive. The website Nutria.com provided recipes and nutritional information. Chef Parola was available for consulting. Food-grade nutria—which is said to taste like dark-meat turkey—was distributed through a local supplier. Louisiana's Wildlife and Fisheries department no longer funds the program, but its ultimate goal, reducing the nutria population, is being met, if the current wetlands-damage tally is an accurate reflection of the situation. The fact that the state is paying four dollars a tail for trapped or shot nutria, eaten or not, isn't hurting either.

Meanwhile, elsewhere in the country, government officials are watching closely. Maryland has a nutria problem, as do other states. In 1998, the U.S. Congress's Subcommittee on Fisheries Conservation, Wildlife and Oceans held hearings specifically related to the situation in Maryland. Rather than eat nutria to beat 'em, Maryland wants to eliminate them without a trace. Testifying before the subcommittee, Dixie Bounds, an assistant unit leader for wildlife research in the Maryland Cooperative Fish and Wildlife Research Unit, said, "We have talked with biologists in Louisiana and they are trying to exploit the restaurant market, trying to make nutria an exotic table cuisine. We've talked about that in our task force and we don't think it would go over well in Maryland . . . there's a strong seafood industry and most folks who visit and vacation on the Eastern Shore want to eat seafood and not rat."

So it looks like "Stuffed Nutria Hindquarters" is unlikely to supplant crab cakes on the Eastern Shore. Down in Louisiana, the nutra rat story continues to unfold.

Ortolan

The most sensually decadent food you'll never eat is ortolan, which in life is a colorful, six-inch-long European migratory bird that is related to the American bobolink. As of August 20, 1999, it has been illegal to hunt, serve, or eat the bird in France or the United Kingdom.

The Brits shrug off this loss, if they've even noticed between chomps on their beloved woodcock and grouse. For the French, however, the ruling came as a gut-punch, striking deep at the Gallic principles of *liberté*, *egalité*, and *gloutonnerie*. Part of the nation's deep cultural attachment for this wee bird came down to its savor, which inspired raptures, examples to follow. But another substantial element of its appeal was the arcane, ritualistic way in which it was eaten, which looked ridiculous to onlookers but to participants bordered on something holy.

Back when it was still possible, a feast of ortolan began in the southwest of France, with the live entrapment of the migrating bird in the months of August and September. Thereafter the ortolan was kept for a month in a dark box (though not deliberately blinded, as it was in ancient days), during which time it was presented with huge portions of grain, berries, grapes, and figs, until it fattened to approximately four ounces, four times its original size. The bird met its end in a vat of Armagnac brandy. The sodden carcass was plucked (but not gutted) prior to cooking. The cooking took place in a very hot oven for a very few minutes, until the bird was just roasted through.

When the cooked birds were brought to the table, the ceremonial draping took place. In a scene reminiscent of an old-time barbershop, or of the beach in Boca on a high-SPF afternoon, the participants draped towels over their faces prior to getting busy with the birdie. For the veiling there are several explanations. The legendary one is that an ortolan-loving French priest did it to hide his indulgence from God, and the practice spread. The fastidious one is that eating ortolan is a dribbly, maw-mouthed process, which a diner would understandably want to keep furtive. The gustatory one is that while tented within the linen towel, the diner was immersed in the steamy fragrance of the freshly cooked bird. The resultant flow of salivary juices protected the tongue from the piping-hot carcass, which was placed whole, unboned, in the mouth, with only the head protruding.

As a next step, the diner decapitated the bird with the incisors, and discarded the head. Chewing was impossible right away; first the diner exhaled heavily around the body to cool it. Once it reached a crunchable temperature, the diner sank his teeth in, "allowing," according to Stewart Lee Allen, author of *In the Devil's Garden*, "its ambrosial fat to cascade freely down [the] throat." At this point, the towel acted as a shade drawn over ecstatic facial expressions.

Since bones and entrails remained intact, it took a while to chew through the birdie. Doing so, in the dark of the towel, the diner was said to experience, again according to Stewart, "the bird's entire life . . . the wheat of Morocco, the salt air of the Mediterranean, the lavender of Provence. The pea-sized lungs and heart, saturated with Armagnac from its drowning, are said to burst in a liqueur-scented flower on the diner's tongue."

Michael Paterniti, author of *Driving Mr. Albert: A Trip Across America with Einstein's Brain*, had a similarly transportive experience eating ortolan. As he describes it, in an article he wrote for *Esquire* magazine, "I am forced to chew and chew again, for what seems like three days. And what happens after chewing for this long—as the mouth full of tastebuds and glands does its work—is that I fall into a trance. I don't taste anything anymore, cease to exist as anything but taste itself. And that's where I want to stay, but I can't because the sweetness of the bird is turning slightly bitter and the bones have announced themselves. When I think about forcing them down my throat, a wave of nausea passes through me. And that's when, with great difficulty, I swallow everything."

Paterniti's article described the starring role the or-

tolan played in former French president François Mitterand's last meal. While it was customary to eat only one
bird per dinner, the leader's advanced cancer and untram-
meled pleasure disposed him to two.

In 1999, with Mitterand firmly ensconced in the Great
Beyond, France made selling the birds a criminal act.

If ortolan were legalized again, how many hard-core
foodies would refuse the chance to throw on a towel?
Few, especially if the birds were given some daylight and
breathing room as they fattened. But it's very unlikely
that the birds' population will ever again reach sufficient
numbers. Foodies must resign themselves to joining the
ranks of misser-outers described by French writer Gri-
mod de La Reyniere, who claimed the ortolan "is prized
even more by those who know only the name than by
those who have tasted it."

Paterniti, one of the ever-dwindling number of people
who have had the pleasure, happens not to agree with
Reyniere. "I feel as if it lived up, in all respects," he says.
Lucky bastard.

Pia

Because the Lao dish *laap* isn't zippy enough, with its
slices of raw water buffalo meat, its bits of cooked liver,
tripe, spleen, and skin, the heaps of scallions, red chilis,

mint, coriander, river herbs, ground roasted rice, and other bits and pieces, the locals like to crank it up—as a Food Network chef might say but in this case would never do, at least on TV—with a special sauce. Its main ingredient is *pia*, the liquid component of digesting matter from within the buffalo's intestinal tract.

The English word for this substance is "chyme." It's important to be specific. The substance is not vomit, for that hasn't taken place. It's not fecal matter, for that transformation occurs a ways—but not much of a ways—down the digestive tract. So chyme it is, an enzymatic wet mulch of the thick wad of grasses that the cow ate for breakfast. Aiding in the digestive process is bile that has dripped down from the gallbladder, bile being an extraordinarily bitter substance that gives this cloudy, dark green liquid its signature flavor.

Pia is widely available in the sprawling rustic market of Vientiane, the capital of Laos. The standard portion is about a cup, sold in a transparent plastic baggy, the ubiquitous market packaging material for liquids in Southeast Asia. At the stall, there is disagreement and debate as to exactly which section of the cow's digestive tract the material comes from.

When posing tricky food-related questions like these, it's always best to ask a group of women of a certain age working in the vicinity of the item. With apologetic bowing, point to it, ask if anybody speaks English, then try to determine what it is, where it comes from, and what exactly about the juice is so all-that that you're charging a buck per baggy? If English is a nonstarter, you could try drawing a sketch, accurate to the extent of your draftsmanship and knowledge of ruminant gastrointestinal anatomy. Fifteen minutes of internecine squabble will follow, for any group of women of a certain age will have individual and strongly held beliefs about the truth of the matter. In the end, whoever speaks the best English or loudest Lao will give or mime her version, with a possible begrudging nod to the other opinions, but not always.

The pia mavens conclude that it comes from somewhere in the buffalo's belly region. Further checks on the deplorably scarce internet source material yield conflicting opinions, but the most likely answer is the duodenum, or the upper portion of the small intestine, which seems logical given the presence of bile, which drips in fairly late in the digestive game. As for the taste of the raw material, it's impossible to say, for the women forbid dipping in a finger, insisting the pia be diluted and boiled first.

Perhaps this is a concession to our more fussy, modern age. In the deserts of Arabia, Bedouins would, as a last resort, slit the stomachs of their camels to drain and drink a similar fluid, which they called *fazz*. It has "a startling green colour and has a strong odour," says R. T. Wilson, author of *The Camel*, but in their situation the Bedouins were beyond caring. Native Americans, for their part, consumed the prairie version of pia with gusto. According to John (Fire) Lame Deer, in his memoir *Lame Deer, Seeker of Visions*:

In the old days we used to eat the guts of the buffalo, making a contest of it, two fellows getting hold of a long piece of intestines from opposite ends, starting chewing toward the middle, seeing who can get there first; that's eating. Those buffalo guts, full of half-fermented, half-digested grass and herbs, you didn't need any pills and vitamins when you swallowed those.

Back at the pia stall at the Vientiane market, the ladies demonstrate via pantomime how it is obtained: the duodenum (or whatever) is strip-squeezed to extract the juice, much as you'd get the last of the hair conditioner out of a freebie foil sample. The product, while teeming with bacteria accrued on its passage through the buffalo's four stomachs, smells overwhelmingly of concentrated fresh-mown grass.

Once it has helped marinate the meat and is dressing the laap, pia can only be discerned by the bitterness it brings to the salad. Somewhat needless to say, laap—with its raw meat, tap-washed greens, aggressive spicing, and near-fecal flavoring component—packs together every food peril known to the Western traveler . . . but it's a nice salad. And if you're willing to take on the risk, sometimes it's worth it to try things that would give the Food Channel's health and safety advisors a huge laugh.

Prickly Pear

When the Spanish explorer Álvar Núñez Cabeza de Vaca was separated from his fleet somewhere near present-day Tampa Bay while scouting new territories for Spain in 1528, thus began the adventure of a lifetime. He was captured by, escaped from, and became a notable figure amid Native American tribes up and down Texas, New Mexico, Arizona, and Mexico. He chronicled his experiences in a sprawling and richly detailed true-life tale. Here he describes his impressions of the Iguaces:

They are a very merry people, and even when famished do not cease to dance and celebrate their feasts and ceremonials. Their best times are when "tunas" (prickly pear fruit) are ripe, because then they have plenty to eat and spend the time in dancing and eating day and night. As long as these tunas last they squeeze and open them and set them to dry. When dried they are put in baskets like figs and kept to be eaten on the way.

Prickly pear fruit is a refreshment so acid-juicy and sweet it instantly drenches a parched throat. Depending on the species and state of ripeness, the flavor is reminiscent of berries, melon, or citrus. The fruit is delicious eaten raw, but may also be used beyond immediate needs: dried, cooked down into a jam, or fermented into the powerful alcohol called *colancha* in Mexico. The flat green pads of prickly pear (actually wide stems) are called *nopales* and they too are good to eat, scraped clean of their spines and cut into ribbons for a salad or lightly cooked side dish. Their flavor is similar to fresh green beans. The flowers that precede the fruit burst into yellow, orange, pink, and red fire in early spring, a spectacle Meriwether Lewis, of the Lewis and Clark expedition, called one of the great beauties of the plains.

So far, so pleasing, these members of the *Opuntia* genus. But the charms are couched behind defenses that give this plant its common name. Spines are a hallmark of cactus, the clear and present danger in its harvest. But the pads and fruit of the prickly pear have another feature that sound less immediately threatening: aureoles. They are dark, soft-looking raised areas surrounding the spines that have a tufty, tactile allure. They look velvety. You kind of want to touch them. And here's what happens if you do.

The brushing contact releases one or more small, fine, almost invisible needles called glochids, which burrow into your skin with a remorseless efficiency, at which point the plant's attraction screeches sharply and shockingly into reverse. Under magnification, the tip of a glochid is icily cruel, bearing not just a hook at the terminal end but barbs running up and down the shaft. A glochid is intelligent design at its most dreadful, and it will defy attempts to remove it. According to research cited in *Botanical Dermatology* by John Mitchell and Arthur Rook, "If an attempt is made to suck the glochids from the skin, they are likely to attach themselves onto the tongue. They may be removed from the skin by spreading an adhesive plaster [bandage] over the area and ripping it off quickly. Melted wax may also be used." Pain begets pain. It's almost as though it were intentional. The book also advises against going near prickly pear when it is windy, for the glochids can become airborne and fly into skin, eyes, or clothing, where they'll lie in wait and get you later. The plant itself seems capable of entrapment. Writer O. Henry describes the peril in his story "The Caballero's Way":

More weird and lonesome than the journey of the Amazonian explorer is the ride of one through a Texas pear flat. With dismal monotony and startling variety the uncanny and multiform shapes of the cacti lift their twisted trunks, and fat, bristly hands to encumber the way. The demon plant, appearing to live without soil or rain, seems to taunt the parched traveller with its lush grey greenness. It warps itself a thousand times about what look to be open and inviting paths, only to lure the rider into blind and impassable spine-defended "bottoms of the bag," leaving him to retreat, if he can, with the points of the compass whirling in his head.

To be lost in the pear is to die almost the death of the thief on the cross, pierced by nails and with grotesque shapes of all the fiends hovering about.

This, an image from the literary imagination, is a home truth for the hapless individuals who, in small numbers every year, fall into cactus patches. Simple puncture wounds from the spines are not the end of the story; they frequently also experience painful rashes and sores, and in severe cases, cancerlike tissue masses arise from the substances in the cactus sap or fungus on the pads, the masses requiring surgical removal.

Authorities seeking to clear stands of prickly pear have learned that the plant sticks in more ways than one. Australians imported several varieties in the nineteenth century as a food source, a fodder, and a garden plant. To say it thrived would be an understatement. In 1886, the government passed its first Prickly-Pear Destruction Act. The act made little impression on the plant, which by 1925 covered some sixty million acres in New South Wales and was spreading at a rate of over a million acres per year. Nothing could stop it, not even the arsenic fumes boiled in the pear stands in an attempt to poison them out of existence. What finally worked, saving Australia from becoming one enormous prickly-pear planter, was the importation of a small caterpillar, cactoblastis, which had a huge appetite for the cactus and chewed it back to livable numbers.

Ponder all this as you eat your nopales salad at the Maria Bonita restaurant in Oaxaca, Mexico. It is hard to believe that such a tender, green-bean-esque vegetable could ever cause such a fuss. Until you take a look at your guidebook, which tells you that the people just up the hillside at the temple complex of Monte Alban would ritually sacrifice victims using cactus pads as the instruments of death. Quick, eat up those nopales. And don't turn your back on them.

Quaq

For many of us, crunching ice, especially the porous crushed ice at the bottom of a soda cup, is a barely registered yet irresistible sensual pleasure, a low-rent granita you didn't pay extra for. Likewise, a Popsicle's best moment is right toward the end, when your teeth plow right through the ice crystals to meet the stick. Frozen grapes, always talked up in women's magazines as a health-conscious alternative to ice cream, are delicious in their own right, especially once they defrost to the point where they yield to the jaws in a slo-mo gush of freezy-sweet saliva.

We'll happily eat a semifrozen dessert or drink (especially if it's served in a tiki mug or a glass with salt on the rim). But that's pretty much where our freezing-temperature tolerance draws to an end. In contrast, the peoples living near the Arctic Circle, partly out of necessity, partly out of ingenuity, eat well beyond this limited range of icebox treats. Foremost among their gelid delicacies is raw meat that is sliced and eaten while still frosty stiff.

The meat in question can be caribou, walrus, seal, whale, fish, or shellfish—the preparation is much the same. Laid down in bitter-cold ambient air as quickly as possible after it's been killed, butchered, and dressed, the meat is flash-frozen in temperatures that, in winter, typically reach −30°F. The cold is literally a cryonic blast, and its benefits as a preservation method are threefold. First, since bacteria can't thrive under these conditions, spoilage is stopped in its tracks. Second, quick-freezing preserves the foods' nutrients better. Third—as exploited by food scientists and the technicians overseeing cryonically preserved dead people who aim to be back once the know-how evolves—the faster tissue is frozen, the smaller the ice crystals that develop within the tissue structure. Smaller ice crystals mean less damage when the cells are allowed to thaw. Where the corpsicles are concerned, this means the potential preservation of function. Where food is concerned, it means optimal preservation of taste and texture.

These benefits did not pass unnoticed by Clarence Birdseye during his younger days as a fur trader in remote Labrador, in 1915. He saw how the indigenous peoples kept stores of food not only edible, but delicious, through the most forbidding days of winter. In 1922, back in the States, he began experimenting with technology that would eventually lead to a frozen-food empire. He also wins a Fierce Food All-Star Team shirt for comments like: "I ate about everything . . . beaver tail, polar bear and lion tenderloin [it's unclear what a lion was doing in Labrador]. And I'll tell you another thing—the front half of a skunk is excellent."

It wasn't just the flash-freezing that has proven so healthful to the Inuit diet, it is also the fact that they don't cook the meat once they pull it out from cold storage. *Quaq*—a term used to describe any quick-frozen, lightly thawed raw meat—loses none of its nutrients to flames or boiling water. (*Eskimo* is reputedly an Algonquin designation meaning "those who eat their meat raw.")

Thanks to this custom, Arctic peoples are often held up as exemplars of the raw-food diet. If veganism, with its avoidance of all things animal, seems a bit slack, the raw-food movement, with its avoidance of all things stove, offers a monastic rigor that nonetheless allows for extreme flights of fancy, just as illuminated manuscripts allowed the talents of cloistered artists to flourish. The movement has long had a core group of devoted followers, but recently it has been embraced on a wider scale by the worlds of fashion and film, as well as by chefs like Thomas Keller and Charlie Trotter, who doubtless appreciate the challenge it poses to their formidable talents. "There are ways to make this food explode with flavor," Trotter told the *New York Times*. Back up north, the characterization of Inuits as arch-raw-foodies is not accurate—they eat plenty of cooked food—but the basic principle that quaq is very healthy holds.

This is a fine reason for quaq to be a northern staple, but there's much more to it than that. Zona Spray Starks, who grew up in arctic Shungnak, Alaska, and now is a cooking expert, wrote about these qualities in a paper for the Oxford Symposium on Food and Cookery:

If food historians understood quaq, they would herald it as a national dish. It pleasures all the senses. Texture, temperature, taste and sound build to an explosive mouthful. The Inupiq word ca-cocktat, meaning food that cracks between the teeth like bone, describes it well. Freezing quaq is simple. Timing the finished product is crucial. While defrosting, an experienced finger presses, testing the surface. When a slight indentation remains, quaq is ready. Neither rock hard nor soft, thousands of tiny ice crystals remain amid partially thawed protein fibers. Quickly the cook cuts slices carpaccio-thin and sends the frosty slices around the room. Dunked in seal oil and popped into mouths, the icy crystals shatter with each bite. Just as quickly they melt; each cut of meat exuding its own unique flavor. Should the thin slices thaw beyond the ca-cocktat stage, a hot seal oil dunking is in order.

Simply put, quaq provides a startling, multitextured, and highly gratifying eating experience—"bursting with flavor" would be an understatement. Can it be long before the world's greatest chefs discover raw-frozen caribou or quaqqed salmon roe—this entire class of traditional Inuit food—as a new way to give their talents a workout?

Salt Licorice

Danes, Swedes, Norwegians, Finns, and the Dutch share a largely sunless winter, buffeted by icy sea winds. They also share a love of a candy so bizarre that its description effectively dismisses it from the category, putting it in a class of its own. There's got to be a connection between climate and confection. Conditions: dark, forbidding, salty. *Why not make candy just like that!* And so salt licorice was born. Which may or may not be the actual birth story. One more bizarre thing about this stuff is that nobody—not even the people who currently make it—can tell you who invented it or why.

The addition of salt transforms the already funky taste of real licorice into a near hallucinogenic clash of oral sensations. At turns searingly sweet, bitingly salty, and smacking of tang, it is confection as S&M experience, pleasure and recoil and disgust and puzzled enslavement all boiled into one. Up against salt licorice, a Twizzler couldn't be straighter. And it's a covert pleasure—the only indication that you've even had it is a tongue gone black as pitch.

Ask a Dane far from home about salt licorice, and *the look* will fall over his face. You see this a lot when you talk to people about strange foods of their homeland. The eyes cast to the left, the lids lower, and a faint smile plays at the lips. You're watching a person deep in reminiscence, reliving a childhood habit. After a moment his eyes will refocus on yours, and he'll whisper, "Got some?"—an ex-junkie ready to freefall back in.

Licorice (a.k.a. liquorice) of the nonsalty variety has been eaten since ancient times. It derives from the dried rootstock of the beany *Glycyrrhiza glabra*, a perennial shrub that grows in the warmer and drier regions of Europe and Asia. Licorice is made by pulverizing the roots and boiling them in water, which yields a syrup that concentrates the glycyrrhizin, a compound that lends the characteristic flavor and sweetness (it is frequently claimed that glycyrrhizin is fifty times sweeter than sugar). Licorice syrup is then further processed into extracts, sticks, or pastes, to simplify its use as a flavoring agent for candy, dark beer, and cigarettes. The rootstock and its derivatives are also widely used as a healing and fortifying agent.

Old-school European manufacturers combine licorice extract with ingredients like molasses, sugar, flour, and gelatin to make candy of varying degrees of sweetness and chew—from the near-acrid, pellet-hard pastilles sold in tins as throat lozenges to the gummy sweets so beloved in countries whose forests are inhabited by elves. American licorice, if it is mass-produced, is unlikely to contain actual licorice at all. Even though the extract has impeccable bloodlines in American confectionary history (Good & Plenty was the first branded candy; Black Jack was the first packaged chewing gum), anise flavoring has largely overtaken glycyrrhizin as the tastemaker of the American product.

Fans of true licorice are unlikely to find it at mass-market retailers, but a remarkable variety is available through the internet, including the aforementioned salty subgroup. In the Nordic countries it is as much a mainstay of national identity as pickled herring and cross-country skiing. In Stockholm, in the very brainy gift shop of the Nobel Museum, are replica sticks of dynamite—in honor of prize founder Alfred Nobel's most noteworthy invention—made from salt licorice. (If you're bringing some home for friends and family, don't pack it in your carry-on luggage, unless a controlled explosion of fake TNT is something you'd find amusing while handcuffed in a little room at the airport. Less controversial is the Wrigley's Extra gum in salt licorice flavor, available throughout Scandinavia.)

Salty licorice has developed into such a broad category that it's possible to buy it with a mere dash of salt (the taste almost negligible, like in salt-water taffy); moving on up to double-salt, which is definitely wacked; and then into the outer fringes of triple salt, which is so stunningly saline it's like chewing licorice while submerged to your nose in the Dead Sea.

It gets weirder still. There's something unusual about the salt itself. This is not the sodium chloride molecule as we know it—it has a laser-sharpness and a petroleum tang that makes mere table salt seem blunt in comparison. It is a chemical half-brother called sal ammoniac, or salmiac, or, in chemical terms, ammonium chloride. It's best not to dwell on where the stuff comes from; formerly harvested from the ashes of camel dung, it is now gleaned as a by-product of gasworks.

In its pure state, salmiac is a fine white crystalline powder. It has no formal addictive properties, but try telling that to the throngs of Finns who attend the Salt

Licorice Gala every year in Helsinki, consuming a hundred kilos of the stuff in between "dancing to extravaganza pop music, salt licorice praise speeches, blindfold tasting competitions and conversations with nice people," explains Jukka Annala, a journalist and author of *Salmiakki*, a book devoted to the subject.

While frequently whimsical-looking, the little black buttons, fish shapes, and *katjes* (cats) actually have health benefits. Sal ammoniac is known within hospital respiratory wards as an expectorant. The body sheds it through the lungs and bronchial lining, hastening the process by producing a loose mucus that is easily coughed up. The lung-clearing action of the cough also brings relief to nagging throat irritation and congestion.

Which may hold the key to the deep and enduring affection the northern European peoples have for salt licorice. Dipping into their bagful in the freezing sleet of December, they're not only snacking, they're not only experiencing a covert, slightly warped pleasure—as likely as not, they're self-medicating.

San-nakji

In the 2003 film *Oldboy*, Oh Dae-su, imprisoned for no apparent reason, chooses his first meal after fifteen years of solitary confinement. "I want to eat a living thing," he tells the beautiful waitress behind the restaurant counter. She gives him a hand-sized live squid. He grabs it, shoves it headfirst past his lips, and proceeds to chew it down, the tentacles swirling like hallucinogenic gray spaghetti as they disappear into his mouth, a lone leg curling forlornly around his nose in a last-ditch effort at self-preservation.

The scene was not shot using special effects. In Cannes, this is considered bravura filmmaking, and in this case it helped win its director a Grand Jury Prize. In restaurants up and down the Korean peninsula, it's considered lunch. *San-nakji*—live squid—is an appetizer of freshly amputated tentacles (or whole live animals) served with a side plate of salad and pickles and a pair of dipping sauces.

The squidly nervous system does not go gentle into the good night, which you discover yourself after ordering it. A plateful arrives: eight ungarnished tentacles chopped into inch-long pieces. The gray-brown skin glistens atop, the suckers file doubly below, and the pure white flesh within shows no sign of vessels or blood. Initially the tentacles seem reassuringly at ease, a throb here, a lazy switch of the attenuated terminal pieces there. But an exploratory stir with chopsticks riles them, sending these multiple amputees into a thrashing frenzy. At this point you're pretty eager to get the show on the road, before you lose your appetite now and forever.

It quickly becomes clear that decisive action with the chopsticks is called for, because the tentacles are slimy and they will try to evade. You've got one, tight, between the tips of your metal sticks. You bring the pinkie-thick segment to your lips. All of a sudden, the cut end farthest away from you whips around and looks you straight in the eye. This is unsettling, to put it mildly. You need to regroup. And at this point you're getting pissed at tentacles that refuse to die, especially the little whippy ones, which are loathsome. You grab another piece, shove it in your mouth, and chew as hard and fast as possible. This is not for humane reasons (thanks to this lunch you're already slated for animal-rights hell). It is for self-preservation reasons. You might want to bolt it down, but it must be thoroughly masticated before swallowing, or else a segment might mosey over to your windpipe, block it, and choke you to death. Finally, it's down.

Or so you thought, until vaguely at first, then more distinctly, you can feel a piece worming around halfway down your throat. At this point you thank God for the salad and pickles, which you cram down to avalanche the squirmy bits into your stomach. You wave the plate away, thoroughly disimpressed with san-nakji. The waiter takes it, then brings it back two minutes later, steamed and mercifully still.

An alternative scenario was described in the *Korea Herald* in 2002:

The man, identified only by his surname, Ha, died Friday afternoon on his way to the hospital after the eight-legged living mollusk clogged his respiratory tract. Doctors later found a living octopus in his respiratory tract. . . . Police said the man, who had been suffering from a stroke since 1984, liked eating live octopuses. Many Koreans enjoy dining on living octopuses, which are usually eaten with vinegar and red pepper paste.

Especially popular in coastal towns, san-nakji is a typical *anju*, or drinking side plate—the Korean version of tapas, something small and savory to have with a drink to batten the alcohol down. Although, in this case, it's the san-nakji that needs battening. If you've ever wondered what it feels like to have a food fight in your own gullet, Korean restaurateurs have something you've got to try.

Scorpion

You've been feeling run-down, and need something to get you back into sorts. Caffeine won't do it, Red Bull won't do it; you need something with kick. Scorpion. Yeah, that's the ticket. The Chinese say there's nothing quite like scorpion when your yang needs some tender loving care.

But where you gonna get it? If you live in the desert and have a pair of boots and loads of patience, you can wait for one to crawl in, like they do in the movies. Or if you're in Guangzhou, China, you could pluck out a couple from one of the seething tubfuls in the Qing Ping market zone. But transporting live scorpions would tax your poor yang beyond repair. No—best to buy them dead and dried. At the medicinal market just around the corner, near Huangsha Dadao Road.

Enter the enclosed alley-way of shops and be swept into the phantasmagorical world of ancient Chinese healing, where antlers and starfish and unidentified gnarly bits and bobs (some of them endangered) are sold by the dry weight, to be steeped or stewed or pulverized into a heal-ing concoction that's taken as casually as we pop a painkiller. Compared to this place, the Walgreen prescrip-tion counter is yawnamundo. But does any of it really work? The answer is manifest in the sheer tonnage of ma-terials available. If people had no faith in their healing properties, there wouldn't be a market in the first place.

The smell in the alleyway is overpowering—dense, fruity, musty, like a grandmother's attic on a humid day. And it *is* humid in here, drip-pingly so, in a way no halfheartedly rotat-ing set of ceiling fans can touch. Down you go along the aisle, eyes caught by the ex-traordinary goods on display: bushels of twisting roots, heaps of dried cuttlefish shin-gled into great stacks, basket upon basket of ginseng in all colors, grades, and sizes. The vendors don't pay much attention to you; if you don't have Asian features you're probably just window shopping. Every once in a while you'll get a halfhearted call to check out someone's wares. But no, you're looking for something special. And haven't found it yet, to your frustration—maybe they're fresh out of scorpion for the first time in five hundred years. Then something in the very last stall catches your eye. Dark coils, piled up in a basket. Snakes, loads of them, dried but still horribly creepy even in their carefully coiled rest. Looking away, your eye lands on another basket. Dark brown, three-inch-long, multilegged creatures, too many legs, so tongue-depressor flat they look like they've been ironed. Centipedes, impaled five to a stick. Still not what you want, but things are looking up. With inventory like this, how could they not stock . . . and there, the second basket near the back. Piles upon piles upon piles of perfectly dried and preserved scorpions, the bulbous tips of the stingers still poised—an inch and a half of golden-yellow menace that sits nice and still in the palm of your hand. You're feeling better already.

Time to start dealing. The young girl with the braces waves you off; she doesn't believe you're serious. Hearing your protests, a crowd of vendors starts to draw near. An older man points to the basket, disbelief all over his face. You nod. You don't speak Cantonese, he doesn't understand Yank, nobody's sure how to proceed. But then you remember the ancient Chinese saying "money talks, bullshit walks," and you take out your wallet. A murmur of approval rises. You flash five yuan. He nods, and you're done.

With a handful of arachnids safely bagged and in your

possession, you're ready to prepare the medicine. The recipe is as follows: Take one bottle of rice wine. Open it and insert the scorpion. Close it. Now let it sit in a dark place for four years.

At the end of the steeping process, the wine will be filled with scorpion, and vice versa. You can now drink, but limit yourself to one glass only, this is powerful stuff. If you can't resist taking a nibble of Mr. Stingy, go ahead, after all this time the poison will have dissipated. It also neutralizes upon cooking. This, by the way, is another, quicker way to take your medicinal scorpion, boiled in a tonic soup for a couple hours.

After this restorative, you feel so good you could practically scuttle.

Sea Cucumber

The sea cucumber easily outdoes its vegetable namesake in terms of interesting talents. Unfortunately, seducing the taste buds isn't one of them. If you haven't grown up eating sea cucumber, a dish like the Eight Immortals Crossing the Sea is unlikely to be the prized feast food for you that it is for your fellow banqueters.

The sea cucumber is related to the starfish and sea urchin, but it looks like a great big slug creeping across reef rocks and the ocean floor. If it's slow going down to the seabed, it's even slower preparing the harvested animal for shipment. An edible species like *Apostichopus japanicus* is readied in a lengthy process involving boiling, slitting it through the back, boiling it again, gutting it, and drying it. What results is a shrunken, desiccated grayish lump that looks like a slug-shaped piece of concrete, with—in some species—ridges of blunt spikes. So transformed, it is shipped to its destination markets. Because of the equally lengthy rehydration process, involving a twelve-hour soak and repeated boilings before the actual cooking takes place, the creature is more often made by restaurants than home cooks. In Cantonese restaurants, it shares menu space with shark-fin soup and bird's nest soup, which also require long soaks before cooking.

Sea cucumber is the star of myriad possible dishes, supported by other sea creatures, vegetables, or meats, depending on the recipe and the ingenuity of the chef. The animal is easy to recognize, even after long braising in oyster sauce: it will be the thick, C-shaped chunks of flesh, brown on the exterior tingeing to a tawny gray within, with a sheen that comes from slimy essence of the creature as much as it does from the cornstarch-thickened sauce.

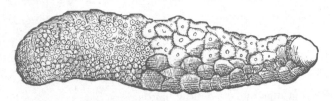

Like jellyfish, sea cucumber is relished in Asia for its texture, which, as it happens, is nothing like jellyfish at all. Jellyfish is crunchy. Sea cucumber is gummy and gooshy; the teeth plow right through, perhaps encountering core material of a more fibrous texture that was not softened thoroughly by the water baths. The closest familiar equivalent is the thick ridge of fat that lies at the edge of a slab of prime rib. As for taste, some diners swear that it has none of its own, taking up the character of the sauce in which it stews, but personal experience may contrarily and repeatedly indicate that the flavor is evocative of what shoe leather might taste like, after it's spent a day covering a foot.

But we can forgive the sea cucumber its less appealing land-bound characteristics, for it is a creature from another world. Down there in home surf, it is devastatingly cool. Indeed, it is way, waaaaayyyy cooler than you.

For starters, there is the animals' class name. It's a holothurian. How wicked is that? It sounds like a being from a galaxy beyond, and easily lives up to the tag. Consider this:

- It can reproduce asexually, which means all alone, which sounds boring, but here means the sea cucumber tears itself in two and regenerates the missing halves.

- It breathes through its anus. This sometimes fools the uneducated aquarium owner of a pet sea cucumber into chatting with the animal's wrong end.

- When food is scarce, the sea cucumber can self-digest. Again, the uneducated aquarium owner might be puzzled as to why his cucumber appears to be shrinking.

- If alarmed (say, by an aquarium owner poking at his incredible shrinking sea cucumber) it can spontaneously eject all of its bodily water, shrinking down to a hard, small pellet.

- If truly scared out of its wits, a sea cucumber can literally puke its guts out, confounding its enemies while it makes its poky escape. As long as conditions are good, it will regenerate the innards if given time and a secure, quiet place.

- A sea cucumber might choose to regenerate its missing parts in the safe confines of a rocky crag. It can fit into a space that bears no relationship to its cylindrical shape because its skin contains a material called mutable collagenous tissue, which will desolidify upon the creature's neural command. In this way, the cucumber can ooze into a cranny, and resolidify once it's inside.

Chinese diners believe that eating sea cucumber will nourish the blood and vital essence, support the healthy action of the kidneys, improve constipation, overcome impotence, and aid longevity. And, yet again, the Chinese appear to be on to something. With survival skills as flamboyant as these, the sea cucumber knows entire chapters about living that we never will.

Sheep's Head

Some say the degree of hospitality shown to guests in the nations of central Asia verges on the insistent. Others say it verges on the pathological. Any way you look at it, you're not going to go hungry (or lack for alcoholic refreshment) at the typical formal dinner in Kazakhstan. Your host will summon plate upon plate of hearty fare because he honestly believes you are too shy to ask for more. Located as you are at some isolated natural gas refinery town or windblown yurt, you are in no position to refuse, nor would you dream of doing so, for this would instantly mark you as a loser beyond hope. This is especially true if the food item in question is the country's national dish, boiled sheep's head. Etiquette requires you to exclaim enthusiastically over the main course's good looks (here, the many rounds of vodka and/or brandy you have already downed will come to your aid). You, as the honored guest, are sure to receive the choicest tidbits. This is a good time to give silent thanks that when she was doling out sheep eyeballs, Mother Nature called it quits at two.

The dish is called *bish pannack*, meaning "five fingers." The mutton flesh has been boiled so long it literally falls off the bone, eliminating the need for cutlery and ensuring that every shred of meat is consumed. Pieces are plated and served in a ritual fashion. You might start out with some slices of cheek — sinewy but flavorful. If children are present, they may receive pieces of ear, so that "they may listen to their elders." Served next is the tongue, so that "you may be a clever speaker." Finally, with the greatest ceremony of all, you are handed an eye, "so that you may see decisions clearly." Now that the many toasts have taken their toll, seeing clearly is probably a dim memory, so just pop the eyeball in and give a good chomp. The inner vitreous fluid will gush, and unless the host has removed it, you may encounter the lens, cooked hard as a stone. The overall sensation has been described as somewhere between a meaty oyster and a rotten grape. If, however, you have any Mongol spirit deep within, you may agree that the taste is truly delectable, and what the hell is wrong with all those eye-averse wusses back home.

If you count yourself among the wusses, look on the bright side. In many countries, sheep's eye is a traditional cure for hangover. This way you've already gotten a head start on what promises to be a baaaa-d morning after.

Silkworm Pupae

Silk's status as luxury good is indisputable. Its appeal is at once ostentatiously public and singularly private, for the look of it speaks riches while it flows whisper-soft against the skin. Silk traders forged a great road across mountains, desert wastes, and hostile tribes in order to clothe popes and kings. Columbus's 1642 journey from Spain was intended to open a sea route to China, to facilitate getting the material. Even today, when researchers create astounding technical fibers in the textile lab, silk is what women want to wear on their wedding day and night.

At the center of this historic industry is a pale, thirty-millimeter-long animal that wants only to get a little sleep. Along with its fellow larvae, it has been diligently eating through trayfuls of mulberry leaves for a full month since hatching. Its silk glands, paired, twisted tubules that run the length of its interior, are gearing up to full output. When the time is right, it will stop eating, inch over to a twig, and begin to extrude superfine filament. In the Chinese species, the line will reach an unbroken one thousand meters, wrapped and rewrapped to create a warm, snug, safe capsule that will shield the worm's metamorphosis into adulthood.

At least that's the theory. Unbeknownst to the caterpillar, sericulture workers are patiently poised waiting for exactly this moment, for this is when the silk can be unraveled and spun into thread. Traditionally, the cocoons are baked to kill the creatures. Then, sixty to seventy are immersed in a hot bath to loosen the filaments' ends. Workers with pinpoint vision find a microthin trailer, then thread it, along with all the other loose ends, into a spindle that untwists the filaments from the cocoons as they bob in the water bath. Watching the filaments ascend and unite is like watching the twining of spiderwebs. As the filament winds down, the cocoon becomes translucent and you can see the animal within.

From another part of the factory comes the rhythmic clackety-clack of old-fashioned wooden hand looms pedaled and pulled to make fine silk cloth. The operator's hands and feet pump in counterpoint. A shuttle shoots back and forth across the weave. A skilled worker can produce a meter of cloth per hour. In the windows, fans swirl, creating currents, but condensation still drips down the glass, the room's heavy fug an inevitable fact of the Thai climate, hardworking limbs, the steaming vats. Suffusing the air is another factor, a smell so sweet and cloying it's practically a reek: the characteristic odor of raw silk that will persist even through weaving and construction and shipment and warehousing and retailing straight into your closet after you've purchased a garment made from it.

Silk is, of course, the primary product of sericulture, but there's another that in its own right is just as important. The cloth will go to clothe the rich. The pupae, naked, their utility spent, will feed the workers; an invaluable source of protein, healthily raised, and processed under relatively sanitary conditions. The animals are widely available in rustic markets in Southeast Asia, where they're typically sold deep-fried, which makes them thrice-cooked, but does not reduce their meatiness. Silkworm pupae are equally favored by cosmopolitan diners: the finest restaurants in Guangdong Province in China serve them as a stir-fried delicacy.

The pupa is interesting to contemplate. Golden yellow, with wings starting to emerge flat behind the head, it is mostly abdomen, ringed into segments. Its new legs are tucked tight under the head assembly. It is betwixt and between, neither worm nor moth, in a state of suspended animation that in its case will never be transcended.

As pupae go, a freshly cooked silkworm makes for pleasant eating. It has an elastic-to-crispy outer skin (depending on how long it's been out of the frying pan) surrounding a dense, mealy, slightly tangy interior. The flavor and mouth sensation evoke a cheese puff, if you're into fine dining, or a slightly soggy Cheez 'n Cracker, if you're not. It also has a distinctly sweet—almost cloying—aftertaste.

We cultivate the silkworm in order to clothe our skin and self-regard. It's only fitting that the animal itself is also eaten and appreciated, rather than discarded as a leftover of the industry it creates.

Snake

It's the end of a long morning filled with sights and sounds so surreal and exotic your head is still spinning. Time to steady yourself with something to eat, and why not try some of the local cuisine? You gesture your order to the cook and patiently wait in line for your plate. Guts are stripped out before your eyes and a live heart beating on somebody's palm has quickly become commonplace.

Your order is ready. Time to sink your teeth into some snake. They always say it tastes like chicken, but they are wrong. The backstrap meat you're tugging away from the spine and pulling off the ribs in skinny strips bears no resemblance to a typical factory-farmed chicken breast. The muscles hug tight to the bone, not yielding easily to your jaws. You can feel how strong it is with your teeth.

The flavor is different too, no matter whether the snake's been deep-fried, simmered in rice wine, or cooked in a stew with fresh cat. It has an undertone of reptile funk, which doesn't let you forget it's cold-blooded. The cold-bloodedness shows up in other ways. One of them is that the beheaded, skinned, and gutted snakes you just saw being butchered must be soaked in brine tubs with a lid tight on top, lest they decide to slither out and crawl away.

The sound
of a school marching band
playing "Celebrate" makes you look up
from your most primordial of lunches and
you get another jolt of dissociation.
You're not on a survival mission

in the jungle. You're not in Taipei's Snake Alley, which is crowded with restaurants selling all manner of serpent. You are somewhere in America's heartland, at one of the rattlesnake roundups held every spring in the South and Southwest. The high-light of all such events is the gathering and display of hundreds, if not thousands, of rattlesnakes coiled and hiss-ing in a large pit. The Sweetwater, Texas, event, which bills itself as the world's largest, typically displays 2,500 pounds' worth of snake every year. Other goings-on at these roundups may include beauty pageants, snake cook-offs, venom-milking displays, and in some cases "daredeviling," a particularly extreme form of snake handling, in which wranglers may wear coiled rattlers on their heads like hats or snuggle down in a sleeping bag filled with a passel of live snakes.

If you're eating snake at one of these events, you're being a bit of a daredevil yourself, and not just be-cause you're trying a new kind of meat. According to a 1994 position paper by the Kansas Herpetological Society, "the majority of snakes being brought into long-standing roundups are being captured using gasoline. . . . Some, in an attempt to appease concerned parties, have switched from gasoline to ammonia." The hunting technique specifically involves shooting a squirt of a noxious substance down a likely snake hole in order to flush the creatures out. This is not good environmental practice. Nor does it do the animals any favors as a table meat. Again, according to the position paper, some of the potentially hazardous components of gasoline include aromatic hydrocarbons, benzene, and other chemicals that are injurious to organs and may cause genetic mutations.

The Humane Society of the United States wastes no words in its opinion of such roundups, calling them "among the most deliberately cruel public events existing today." So if you have a hankering for snake, you might consider seeking out a restaurant whose suppliers obtain snake in a clean way. The meat might not be as tough a wrestle as the roundup variety, and you don't get a beauty pageant as a sideshow, but at least the meat hasn't been marinated with anything more volatile than venom before it lands on your plate.

Snapping Turtle

Turtle soup used to be much more popular in the United States than it is today. In the wealthy household, the kitchen staff would prepare an enormous tureen as the traditional first course for a gala dinner. Far away from the Main Line, rustic folk would catch an animal from the wetlands, butcher it out back, and serve an equally tasty stew out of rough bowls on an unadorned kitchen table.

Today, in terms of kitchen help, most of us live more like the latter than the former, and we are less disposed to cutting up a critter in the backyard when it's so much easier to open a box of pizza.

Of course, once the turtle is caught and killed and the bony plastron (belly shell) is unhinged and lifted, it *is* kind of like opening a pizza box, at least in terms of the visuals, but we're getting ahead of ourselves. First, there's the matter of finding the creature.

The common snapping turtle (*Chelydra serpentina*) and the alligator snapper (*Macroclemys temminckii*), which reside in ponds, rivers, and lakes all along the eastern two-thirds of the United States, are cooking turtles par excellence, because the largest among them can reach 180 pounds in weight. This is a lot of turtle, as big across as a dartboard. In popular legend they've grown even bigger. Oscar, the Beast of 'Busco, a snapper allegedly sighted in a lake in Churubusco, Indiana, first in 1898, then in 1948, was said to be six feet long and weighing in the neighborhood of four hundred pounds. Despite his vast dimensions, Oscar has never been photographed, much less hauled in, but his legend lives on in the Turtle Days Festival in Churubusco every June.

If there is an element of truth to Oscar's story, it is that snapping turtles are elusive creatures. Hundreds can live in a lake, but the official minutes of the residents' association wouldn't record a single sighting. The animals are largely nocturnal. During the day, the only indication that they exist at all is the sporadic disappearance of small waterfowl paddling on the surface. By and large, the turtles roam (or, more accurately, lumber) the shores by night—in migration, perhaps, if their streambed has dried up, or on the lonely trek off to lay eggs. This is also their preferred time for aquatic hunting, the prey being fish, frogs, crayfish, and other smaller edibles. With the sunrise they return to their muddy hidey-holes by water's edge—in abandoned muskrat burrows, beneath overhanging root systems, or in eroded places within the banks.

Their habits make the animals a challenge to catch (in those states where snapper hunting is still legal). One of the more rough-and-ready methods, called "noodling," involves shoving a foot into a likely bankside hole. If the foot strikes shell, the noodler rummages around for the animal's tail with his hand. The method bears risks. Snapping turtles have not earned their name for nothing. If the wrong end of the animal is grabbed, the hunter's noodling days are over, unless he can adjust to working with the nondominant hand, or with a water-resistant artificial limb. There are countless tales of snapping turtles biting broom handles in half. Whether their jaws are actually that strong is a matter of dispute, but they are absolutely capable of rearing their head back like a snake and striking with the speed of lightning, the neck extending half the length of the carapace.

To put it plainly: a happy-go-lucky snap-per is not a

pretty sight. A pissed-off one is outright terrifying. To behold it is to see the Jurassic in action: the snakelike head with the teeny porcine nostrils, the beaked upper lip, the wormlike tongue (used as a fishing lure in happier times but now vibrating with the furious creature's hisses), the nasty wartlike growths that cover the skin, the fearsome claws, the stink it emits from alarmed glands . . .

If you think the horror subsides once the creature has been safely noodled, hooked, or trapped, think again. First, there's killing it. Then there's cleaning it. Finally, there's dismembering it. From here on in, parental guidance is suggested.

Killing a snapper is, by all accounts, relatively simple, so long as you have a stomach of iron. A stout stick is waved before the animal's gaping, drooling, snapping jaws. Once it clamps down on the bait, it will not let go, so you are free to stretch out the neck to full extension, and chop off the head with a sharp hatchet. The neck, according to recipes, is good eating, so it would be a shame to cut too far down, although hatchet accuracy at this juncture would be largely a matter of luck or practice. Once the animal is dispatched, the novice snapper slayer may be tempted to relax. This is a mistake. The head, though decapitated, is still fully willing and able to inflict a serious bite, and this remains the case, at least according to folklore, until sundown. Likewise, the headless body will plod away from the scene, trying to find the lake. The best way to prevent this is to hang the turtle upside down so that it bleeds out through the neck, hurrying the process of demise. But take care while hanging the turtle, because those still-raking claws can do serious damage.

Once the turtle has stopped moving, it's time to clean it. Old-time recipes specify using a stiff brush, dish soap, and fresh running water. With the brush and detergent, scrub away the algae and any leeches from the animal's shell and skin, then rinse thoroughly with cool water. The animal should be parboiled for about an hour in a huge vat.

After the turtle has cooled, it's time to remove the lower shell. This is accomplished by turning the turtle on its back and sawing (or cutting with a heavy knife) through the solid sections between the legs. The legs and neck should be skinned, and the meat chopped. The liver is also edible, though the gallbladder, a small yellow sac by the liver, should be discarded, as should any fat, which will give the meat a foul flavor.

Now the turtle can be prepared like any other meat: fried, roasted, or, best of all, made into an elegant, sherry-flavored soup or stew for honored guests. They will remark that it is delicious, the chewy fibers shredding like pulled pork that has benefited from cooking for the better part of a day. Best to keep your guests out of the back-yard, though, unless you've cleaned up thoroughly. If they see the packaging of the main ingredient, their appetite might suddenly go missing.

Surströmming

☹ ⧘

Christopher Mellqvist, the young, keen manager of the food hall in Stockholm's NK department store, beams with pride as he explains *surströmming*, a signature dish of his home country. "One time they had a surströmming party in the indoor hockey rink I practiced in as a kid," he says. "For the whole week after, the smell was so bad we felt sick every time we skated."

Surströmming is a picnic food, even if it's October. For eating this canned product indoors, even in a freezing-cold sixty-meter-long hockey rink, delivers a nasal slap shot that lingers for days. Even in blustery October, Swedes won't open the can in the air: instead they'll submerge it in a bucket of water, to help keep the Brownian motion of its unspeakable molecules contained in another medium.

Surströmming translates literally as "sour herring." It translates accurately as "rotten herring, in a can." Any home economics expert will tell you that a bulging canned good is a health risk that should be avoided or, better yet, handed with tuts of disapproval to the store manager. Unless, of course, it's a can of surströmming. The Swedes like to see theirs straining close to spheroid. It's a sign that the contents are ripe; so is the effervescent fizz that tickles the hand of the brave opener.

When asked if airplane transport was safe, manager Christopher's face grew concerned. "How long?" was his first question. When told a couple hours, he pressed further, "In the cabin?" When he was assured yes, it would be carried under pressurized conditions, his features relaxed. "It *should* be OK," he said. "But there is always a small chance that the can could explode."

Surströmming's origins are in northern Sweden. There, an overabundance of fish caught from the summer trawling in the Baltic Sea disposes local residents to store it in brine at 65°F for a month or so. The whole fish is then canned, bones, guts, and all, and allowed to "mature." The contents are typically eaten in late summer or early fall a year later, at festive gatherings involving copious amounts of beer, aquavit, or vodka. "Be sure to eat it by December," said the saleswoman at NK's surströmming counter, pointing to the use-by date. When asked if it would go bad, she could barely hide her astonishment at the wrongheadedness of the question. "No," she said, echoing the manager's warning. "If you leave it too long the can could explode."

To eat surströmming in an authentic fashion, you take a thin slice of local wrap bread (called *tünbrodd*) and thickly slather it with butter. Then add a slice of boiled potato and a slice of raw onion (which in this instance acts as a breath freshener). Once the can is open, and the initial shock wave of head-whacking shitty stench has somewhat dispersed, a chunk is wrapped up in the sandwich. The fish looks like ordinary herring—glistening silver on the outside, brick red within—but to the teeth it is flabby, well along in the process of decomposition. And to the tastebuds . . . while actual feces are not used in the manufacturing process, their essence somehow materializes, along with the taste of bad fish, salt, and pickling vinegar. *Skål!*

For those for whom a mere meal of surströmming isn't enough, it is possible to make a pilgrimage to its spiritual home. This is the tiny Swedish fishing village of Skeppsmalen, outside the somewhat larger town of Örnsköldsvik. Skeppsmalen is so cute and so Ur-northern Swedish it has been declared a Unesco World Heritage site. Since it's not far from the Arctic Circle, if you go in winter, don't be surprised if the sun gets up much later than you do, meaning noon. Not far from the chapel (everything here is not far from the chapel) is the Fiskevistet Surströmmingsmuseet, a small but sturdily funded institution dedicated to the exaltation of the fishing and preservation of Baltic herring. Just out the front door of the museum stands an old-fashioned wooden barrel with SNIFF O MAT painted on its exterior. It offers a head-clearing blast of fermented herring that focuses the mind on the curatorial delights to come.

Surströmming is not without its aftereffects: stinky fingers, bad breath, drunken stupor, vile burps, the possibility of small bones lodged in the throat. The Swedes wouldn't have it any other way. It is their heritage, stamped by Unesco, no less. Secretly, they're not terribly unhappy that exporting cans via airplane offers a small but significant risk of explosion.

Tarantula

While "giant tarantula" might seem redundant, this is indeed the common name of the *Theraphosa blondi* species, native to the tropics of northeastern South America. This spider is more colorfully known as the goliath birdeater, a slight exaggeration only in that the creature prefers to eat large insects and frogs. Which it easily snags, given its legspan of thirty centimeters across—about as big as your face.

You'd think that anything as big and formidable as a giant tarantula wouldn't need defenses more scary than simply popping into view, but that's only the beginning of its capabilities. When it's time to intimidate, the spider threatens would-be aggressors by rubbing together the long thick hairs on its legs, which makes a hissing noise technically known as stridulation.

Anyone who has been out in nature or has watched the shows knows that hissing is bad news. But there are always some rookie aggressors out there in the jungle, along with some dull-witted creatures that never learn. They are about to get a lesson in whup-ass, spider-style. The giant tarantula goes from defense to offense by kicking hairs off its abdomen with its hind legs. "This," says tarantula expert Rick West, "sends the extremely fine hairs (like fiberglass wool) floating into the air towards their aggressor."

The specialized abdominal hairs, for their part, are barbed and irritating, causing respiratory distress or a rashy eruption on the skin (and eyes) if they lodge. Some experts warn that if you see bald patches on a tarantula's abdomen, you know it's a hair-kicker, so you need to be especially nice to it. As if needle-sharp missiles weren't enough of a defense system, the giant tarantula has further resources when the battle comes close. These are the scimitar-like 2.5-centimeter mandibles that the spider plunges into soft flesh, like Count Dracula working an Anne Rice fan club.

Lovemaking does not mellow the lady tarantula. Her aggressive tendencies are merely redirected at would-be suitors. For his part, the male is calm, cool, and kitted out like James Bond after a visit to Q's lab. Some males pack a special clamping device that prevents the female from using her fanglike mandibles while they are doing the deed. The deed, by the way, barely seems worth the risk: the male spider releases preejected sperm from turkey-baster-like bulbs on his pedipalps, which are front-leg-like appendages. His gratification may be minimal, but he usually gets away intact, in contrast to the tragic outcome of most spider sex.

Which, by the way, deserves its own book, or better yet, an animated film. The following anecdotes have nothing to do with the giant tarantula per se, but deserve mention if only to buoy the confidence of female readers in search of empowering role models (with many thanks to the source SZGDocent.org).

1. The female wolf spider will not allow a male to mate with her unless he brings her a present, preferably an insect wrapped in silk.

2. Female *Argiope* spiders always tie their males up. The males hardly ever last past two matings.

3. *Linyphiid* males have special, useless, bulging parts that the female can bite while mating.

4. The golden orb web male spider is so tiny he can jump in for a quickie without the female spider noticing.

5. The red-backed spider essentially says "the hell with it" and throws himself into his mate's jaws midway through the act, totally eliminating that awkward parting scenario where he mumbles something about calling her.

So the giant tarantula has, in comparison, a relatively sane sex life, but there is that other small problem of the Piaroa Indians, who also live in southern Venezuela. The Piaroa like to roast these spiders (after luring them from their burrows by tapping the ground with a stick, imitating the footfall of another spider). The arachnids are also important to this people's spiritual activities. Nick Gordon, who was the filmmaker behind *Giant Tarantula*, describes his impressions of eating *Theraphosa* in his book *Tarantulas, Marmosets, and Other Stories: An Amazon Diary*:

Lunch was about to be served. The two formidable fangs were removed and kept to one side, the large abdomen was twisted off and the contents squeezed out onto a leaf. A large blob of grey and yellow slime oozed out, containing about 40 eggs. The leaf was then wrapped parcel-fashion and placed in the hot ashes at the edge of the fire for a couple minutes. When cooked a miniature omelette was the effect. I found the taste bitter and horrible, but I was extremely hungry.

Then the rest of the spider was put over the flames to roast for a few minutes and then was eaten in exactly the same way as a crab. This was delicious. It was fiddly to get the meat out but it was crab-like in texture and, I thought, tasty. The hunters ate theirs quickly but we approached ours a little more timidly. The shaman then picked up one of the tarantulas' fangs that had been put to one side and used it as a toothpick!

Rick West, the scientific consultant on this film, also took part in this leggy feast. "My impression was that the hard-boiled abdominal contents were bitter, gritty, and unpleasant while the legs, jaws and head tasted like smoky prawn meat and was very tasty—for a spider."

A word of warning: if you are sampling any of the 883 known species of tarantula (in Venezuela or Cambodia or Papua New Guinea, among other places they're served) try to ascertain that the abdominal hairs have been thoroughly singed off by the fire or, if it was cooked in a kitchen, with a blowtorch or similar apparatus. In 2001, the *Internet Journal of Medical Toxicology* reported on an exotic dinner in which tarantulas were served. Diners experienced irritation of the throat, due, the article concludes, to the spiders' incompletely removed hairs (this, by the way, is not a problem with old-world tarantula species, which do not possess such hairs). The article goes on to say "improperly prepared tarantula may be an irritating food. Physicians of patients who consume tarantulas should be aware of this potentially adverse effect."

An additional heads up to physicians: if you're not based in a New World rain forest and your patient is eating tarantulas, sharpen your pencil. The symptoms are unlikely to stop at throat irritation.

Uni

✂ 📖

"Meltingly soft" is not a description people commonly associate with sea urchins, especially unwary bathers who happen to land on one with a bare sole. Spiny, bristling, menacing is more like it, and this is the reputation the sea urchin prefers. It wants us to keep our distance, unaware that inside its shell is some of the most tender, rich, and transportive food in the world.

Actually, this is exaggerating the urchin's brainpower. What it really wants is to eat, excrete, spawn, repeat. Unmolested. Nature took care of the rest, by giving it a physique that looks like a medieval instrument of war.

The most commonly eaten species, the large red urchin *Strongylocentrotus franciscanus*, has spikes growing to about two centimeters long. What's amazing about the spikes is their mobility: they can swivel. Attached to the globular shell with ball-and-socket joints, they swirl on hair triggers to meet a potential source of attack. They work in tandem with rows and rows of tubular feet, which, when fully inflated with water, extend past the spikes. While called feet, and used for ambulation and suction, they also act as hands, catching pieces of food and passing it down around the body to the oral cavity, which opens at bottom center of the animal. Here five jaws converge, like the port of a sci-fi spaceship, to grind incoming kelp and other nutritionals. The urchin's only undefended area, its weak spot, is a ring of soft tissue around the mouth, called the peristomal membrane.

All of the sea urchin's exterior defenses are fixed on protecting its interior resources, which are its progeny. They are stored as eggs or sperm in five gonads—bright yellow or orange tongue-shaped organs arrayed like an asterisk in the top half of the globe. Just before spawning, these sex organs can amount to one-quarter of the animal's total body weight. Like all living creatures, the urchin's existence is an exercise in propagation, but unlike others among us, it has no side interests. Like, say, devoting serious time and money to finding the freshest possible *uni* at a top sushi restaurant.

Uni is Japanese for "sea urchin gonads." The word is not gender specific, for we eat both the male and the female parts. At a top-flight Japanese restaurant in the United States, it's possible the uni comes from waters off Hokkaido. But some of the world's greatest uni is found off the California coast, and there is also significant harvesting taking place in Maine.

Wherever their home waters, the animals are raked from the ocean floor and sent on to coastal processing plants. The work of opening an urchin without damaging the uni or impaling the hand is, needless to say, skilled. Processors are equipped with a pair of spike-nosed, spring-action pliers that open when the handles are squeezed. The pliers are jammed into the creature's soft spot and the jaws are sprung, splitting the shell neatly in two. Workers using long spoons or spatulas delicately extract the uni leaves, then carefully wash them clean of membranes. A quick bath in alum tightens the uni up, enabling it to withstand packing (in beautiful small wooden boxes encased within larger refrigerated boxes) and shipment. The goal is to have the uni in a restaurant within two or so days of harvesting (most supermarket fish has been out of the water for at least a week).

Even after its firming-up bath, so fragile is this organic material that it liquefies at the slightest unnecessary roughness. It literally melts atop the tongue, releasing a flavor described by more than one writer as orgasmic. Fine, fresh uni holds only a whisper of brine, and no fishy flavor or iodine. Instead, it has the consistency and taste of custard that's been flavored with slightly sweet, milky coffee. Like custard, it coats the tongue in an unctuous way—simply from its texture you can tell it is rich in cholesterol, a gram containing nearly twice as much as the equivalent amount of egg yolk.

Most people know uni in sushi form, cuffed with a nori seaweed wrapper atop a rice pontoon. Purists might say that slightly soggy nori will undermine the taste and texture; better to enjoy uni otherwise unadorned on a bed of rice. But the truly militant would argue that it's impossible to get great uni in a restaurant setting, it must be eaten fresh off the reef, preferably on the boat or beach. Along the Senegal coast, people roast urchins in a fire until the spines fall off and the shell is easily cracked. Others elsewhere — Mexico, the French Riviera — are more impatient, wedging a knife into the peristomal membrane and levering it to crack the still-dripping animal apart. It's a brutal operation, but that's how nature works. We've found its weak spot because it found ours.

Yuba

After removing your shoes in the entryway, you pad down the stone path alongside a clear, shallow brook, which ripples over an immaculate gravel bed. A tiny bridge over the brook leads to your quarters, the private tatami room where your lunch will be served. Your escort, a lovely young woman in an ornate silk kimono and obi sash, does not tell you her name and that she'll be your server today. She does not tell you anything, simply inclines gracefully toward the entry, as supple as a willow branch. You duck past the sliding paper door and enter a small room, the floor around the sunken table covered with woven rush tatami mats, the walls paneled in golden wood. All is spare yet beautifully proportioned. An alcove holds a burst of peonies in a simple celadon vase. Opposite is a shelf supporting a trio of rustic earthenware bowls, whose humility belies the fact that each one is probably worth more than your air ticket to Tokyo. The waitress brings a mug of brown tea, which has distinctively Japanese, toasted-wheat overtones. The seemingly artless grace of the room, the absolute deference of the hostess, the sound of the brook beyond the paper door—all are irresistible inducements to relax into your surroundings.

You could be in a *ryokan*, a rustic inn, in the mountains of Japan. Instead you're five floors up in the bustling Ginza district of Tokyo. The Umenohana restaurant is reknowned for its preparations of tofu and *yuba*, thin sheets of bean curd skin. The food presented here bears as much relation to supermarket tofu as a fresh French éclair does to a Twinkie.

In Japan, bean curd is oftentimes an artisanal product. At its simplest, the food—brought to the country from China by Buddhist monks two thousand years ago—is made by soaking, pureeing, boiling, and filtering soybeans. The resulting liquid—*gojiu*, or soy milk—is thickened with one of several natural agents, then pressed under weights to help extract excess water to make tofu. A *New Yorker* article by Judith Thurman presents the cult of *∂ofu* in detail, describing a variation crafted by Yasuie Ishii of Kyoto, who uses organic soybeans, coral-reef-sourced seawater, and lava-block weights to create a product so refined it costs fifty dollars for a large mouthful and is a special treat even at the Japanese emperor's palace.

At Umenohana (which also has a branch in Beverly Hills), bean-curd skin can be had in one of many incarnations, including yuba in a small wooden pail, and yuba shabu-shabu (cooked in a hot pot of boiling water). But you have come for another variation—one that is formed by the elements as you watch, and then, when it reaches its ultimate state of readiness, taken by you and eaten.

Hikiage yuba is one of the most extraordinary dishes ever concocted. It is a sheet of just-set bean-curd skin that is skimmed off the surface of a pot of boiling soy milk. Ordinarily, this sort of film, of the same sort that forms on the surface of scalded milk or a very old cup of coffee, is repulsive. Here it transcends its mien of scummy neglect and becomes a food ethereal in its delicacy and deeply warming in its essential goodness.

After you've had a few minutes alone with your tea, the waitress returns, fires the built-in burner in the center of the table, and brings in a foot-square metal container nearly filled to the brim with cream-colored soy milk. This is the gojiu, set down on the burner to heat. She next lays out a large bowl of soy sauce; a small dish holding a lime, a grater, and a small wooden brush; and a pair of extra-long chopsticks, and departs. After a few minutes, steam begins to rise from the container, filling the room with even more sensual atmospherics. Puckered wrinkles begin to appear on the surface of the liquid; the skin is beginning to form. After about ten minutes, it will be ready to skim.

In the meantime you have prepared your dipping

sauce, a ritual unto itself. Grate a smattering of lime peel into the empty cup provided on the table, the volatile oils zinging into the steamy air. To the lime add a dash of soy sauce. To take the hikiage yuba: With the long chopsticks, tease a tip of the skin away from a corner of the metal container, gently lift it, and drop it into the center—as though you were doing origami with a very thin, very pliable sheet. Continue with the remaining three corners so that the result is a bundle of skin floating in the center of the container. Grasp the bundle carefully (it's slippery). Dip it into the cup holding the soy sauce and grated lime peel. Flip your chopsticks (in any formal dining situation in Japan that involves a communal pot, so it's good manners to use the blunt ends for manipulating your food in and out of the pot, and the pointed ends to actually eat). Lift the hikiage yuba dripping to the mouth, and eat.

In flavor, it most closely resembles a slightly sweet, slippery, ultrathin ravioli or wonton that has lost its filling. It is mainly a medium for the lime-soy dipping sauce, which turns slightly milky with the added drips of gojiu. When the yuba has been largely skimmed from the container, you will find, in the bottom, a reddish layer of the so-called sweet yuba, which has even greater intensity of flavor. It and its precursor are wholesome, light, and yet deeply warming. It is the food equivalent of a goose-down duvet.